Falling into Your Purpose

5 Powerful Testimonies of Turning Tragedy Into Triumph

Sophia Janell Taylor

Also by Sophia Janell Taylor

Faithful Liar

Honest Deception

Ruthless Saint

Falling Into Your Purpose
ISBN 978-0-9859338-9-0

Copyright © 2017 by Sophia Janell Taylor
Requests for information on ordering, scheduling the author for signings and appearances should be addressed to: sagaciouspublishing@yahoo.com

All right reserved. No part of this publication may be reproduced in any form or by any means, including electronic, without mechanical or photocopying or stored in a retrieval system or transmitted without permission in writing form Sagacious Publishing, LLC, except for brief passages to be included in reviews.

Cover Design by:
Conkreteworks.com
Editor: Julie Deadrick & Lottie Ferguson
Paperback book and ebook format by:
Sandra Peoples, Publishing Consultant
coachsand@gmail.com

Contents

INTRODUCTION	VII
DEDICATION	VIII
ACKNOWLEDGMENTS	IX
DEDICATION II	XI
ONE	1
CIRCUMSTANCES VS. DETERMINATION	1
TWO	24
LETTING GO	24
THREE	46
CHOOSING YOU	46

FOUR 64

PLAYING THE HAND I WAS DEALT 64

FIVE 80

SEARCHING FOR ANSWERS 80

F.I.Y.P WORKBOOK QUESTIONS 2

ABOUT THE AUTHOR 33

INTRODUCTION

Do you know what it's like to be stripped of your mobility, finances, confidence, freedom, innocence, self worth and regular lifestyle?

Have you ever experienced something so debilitating that you couldn't imagine recovering? I have and so have the people in this book.

With great honor I bring you testimonials from everyday people that turned life's trials into triumphs. Like many they've experienced 'faith testing' situations.

From physical ailments, family tragedies, financial catastrophe's, addictions, abuse, depression and everything in between.

I'll take you on their journey during their highest of highs and lowest of lows. I'll show you the steps they took to turn their lives around and offer tools for you to do the same. These testimonies prove the saying to be true.

It's not how you fall. It's how you rise!

DEDICATION

    This book is dedicated to my Mother and Father. Thank you for never demanding that I move the way the world says I should.

    What flows from my mind and out of my fingertips is the evidence of two people that cared enough to try. You are the reason I dance to a different beat.

ACKNOWLEDGMENTS

God has been the anchor in the most tumultuous times of my life. He speaks and works through people near and dear to me. Writing has been such a gift from God and I'm grateful beyond words to be the vessel for this project. I am proof that anything is possible.

To Julie, Lottie, J. Hump, and Sandra, your patience and knowledge have carried me further than you could ever imagine. Thank you.

Thank you for putting the (art) in graphics A.D. Hester. To Tynisha Howell, Cherisse Bradley , Wantaz Davis, A. Lathan, and everyone else that opened their soul and allowed life to flow out and humbly into me. I appreciate the survivor in you. Thank you for your courage and for adding to my purpose.

To my support system. Thank you all for pushing me to continue encouraging others, your acknowledgment for this mission means more to me than you can imagine. I have the best circle surrounding me and I'm grateful for each and every one of you.

To my family and friends, thank you for putting up with me and my many voices. Each and every one of us loves you. ;-)

The mere fact that my ninety six year old grandmother unapologetically says whatever comes to her mind encourages me to do the same. I love you Gamma.

Finally, to the city that planted seeds in me that fought to grow, I am a proud product of you. Like water flowing through the stream, Flint, Michigan will carry out the dream.

Trust me, we will rise and thrive again.

DEDICATION II

For every time you've shared pieces of your life with me, my spirit was right there with you.

Thank you for your contribution and your candor.

I pray that love, laughter, health, wholeness, passion, purpose and God's total peace forever consumes you.

This book is dedicated to the broken and the healed. To the lost and found and to those that still struggle with the question "why me?"

Hopefully this will help.

Falling Into Your Purpose

Turning Tragedy Into Triumph!

ONE
CIRCUMSTANCES VS. DETERMINATION

Circumstances should never forecast your destiny.

Determination should...

I remember like it was yesterday. I lay on the floor covering my head praying for the shots to end.

"Please make it stop. God please, make it stop." Then just like that, they did.

The sudden ceasing of gunfire gave me reason to fear that footsteps would soon follow and enter our apartment. I figured whoever had balls enough to shoot up a building would surely come inside to complete the job. My heart beat wildly from fear of the unknown.

"Is this it?"

"Is this how my life is gonna end?"

Sophia Janell Taylor

My eyes took mental snapshots of all the shattered items recklessly shuffled on the floor. Only moments ago, like us, they were all intact.

Within those few minutes, more damage had been done than a lifetime of good. It was so unreal. I literally felt like I was inside of a nightmare and all I wanted to do was wake up.

At 22 years young the world was my oyster. I had everything going for me. I'd just signed up for school and was working two jobs. I was also modeling in fashion shows and writing poetry, which later ignited my passion for performing on stage. I found myself drawn to anything that involved artistic expression.

I'd been living on my own since the age of 18 and I loved it. I'm the kind of person that has to have freedom. If restricted in any kind of way, I feel like I'm suffocating. Unfortunately I'd hit a snag and had to move back with my mother and wasn't too happy about it. Needless to say, not long after moving back I began looking for my own place.

I filled out rental applications everywhere, but they all denied me saying that I didn't meet their financial requirements. My mother knows me so well. She could sense my urgency to move, yet encouraged me to relax and continue saving money until the right place came up, but silly me, I wouldn't listen. Freedom kept screaming my name.

As fate would have it, my supervisor's daughter told me that she was relocating and offered me the opportunity to sublet her apartment. It was a no brainer for me. It was affordable and there were no hoops to jump through. The offer was God-sent, I figured. Strangely enough, my mother had reservations. I tried calming her uneasiness by

Falling Into Your Purpose

reassuring her that everything would be fine, but her intuition gnawed at her. Adding to her reservations was my boyfriend at the time. He felt the same as my mother. He thought I should stay at home a bit longer and wait for the right place to come through.

I ignored them both and followed my cries for independence. The lady's offer became sweeter the day she called telling me that I could move in much earlier than expected. Not long after, my cousin and I excitedly moved into the apartment, and once again it felt good to have my own place.

A couple of weeks after we'd moved in, I stopped by my moms to pick up my mail and chat with her a bit. During our conversation she suggested that I stay the night with her. I contemplated it, but realized that I had to pick my cousin up from work and take her to the apartment. I would then have to turn around and drive all the way back to my mother's house. After weighing the back and forth, I declined her invite and told her that I'd sleep over some other night.

Hours later I picked my cousin up from work then we hung out a bit. We returned home around 1 a.m. Neither of us felt sleepy, so we stayed downstairs watching television. We were sitting on the couch and I couldn't help but hear her fussing with her friend on the cell phone. I grew tired of their bickering and told her to let me speak with him. She ignored me and continued arguing with him until the phone went silent. Apparently he had hung up on her. Soon after, her phone rang again. I held my hand out demanding that she give me the phone.

"Let me talk to him. Give me the phone." I said. She ignored me and answered it anyway. I watched her facial expression change suddenly and wondered what he could've said to her to make her demeanor switch so drastically. I held my hand out again demanding to talk to him.

"Let me talk to him!" I said more aggressively.

She removed the phone from her ear and looked over at me like she'd seen a ghost.

"What did he say to you?" I asked her.

"Whoever that was said 'you've got until tomorrow night to get the hell out of that house.'" At first I thought she was joking.

"Quit playing!"

"Do I look like I'm playing?" She responded.

It was obvious that she didn't recognize the voice on the other end because she didn't crack a smile. In fact, I'd never seen her look more serious.

My cousin purchased the phone she was using from the person we'd sublet the apartment from a week prior to us moving in. The lady said she was selling it because it only offered local service. After moving out of the apartment, she planned on relocating to another state. She gave specific instructions to my cousin to tell anyone that called for her that she was the new owner of the phone and that she didn't know anything else.

After receiving such a disturbing call, I got up and walked into the kitchen. I made a call to another family member that also happened to be close with the lease holder. I told him about the call we'd just received then he began shedding light on what he thought the call could've been about. He brought me up to speed, telling me that she'd been involved in a nasty altercation before we moved in but told me not to worry because more than likely nothing would come of it.

Falling Into Your Purpose

"More than likely!" I thought to myself. I couldn't believe they allowed us to move in knowing that there was drama lurking nearby. I hung up the phone and walked back into the living room.

"Let's go," I said to my cousin. It didn't take much convincing. She was already putting her shoes on. I was about to follow suit but the gunfire sent me flying to the floor. Within seconds our apartment became a war zone.

The shattering glass, rapid gunfire and the bricks breaking off of the building left me no choice but to take cover and pray. The sounds and the force were so overwhelming! It felt like 50 people were outside shooting at our building.

I followed my first instinct and hit the ground. My second instinct was to make sure my cousin was alright. From the floor in mid ambush, I turned to locate her and realized that she was still sitting on the couch. She looked frozen like she was in too much shock to move. I jumped up and snatched her down to the ground then resumed my position on the floor.

"Please make it stop. God please make it stop," I prayed to myself from the floor. After what felt like forever, the gunfire ceased. I looked around to make sure she was okay. I would've never lived it down if something had happened to her while she was with me.

"Call the police!" I shouted to her from the floor. "Call the police!"

I went to stand up but the pressure from something heavy on my legs hindered my movement. I kept trying to push it off but it wouldn't budge.

"Get that off of my legs!"

I tried with all of my might to push it off but I couldn't.

Sophia Janell Taylor

"Get that off of my legs!" I shouted to her again.
"Ty, there's nothing on your legs," she responded.
"Yes there is, just get it off of me so I can get up!"
"There's nothing on your legs, Ty!" she repeated.
"Oh my God you've been shot! Ty you've been shot!"

I didn't feel any pain so I knew she had to be mistaken.

"No I haven't! Just get that off of me!"

I reached my hand around to touch my back then brought it back towards my face. And that's when I lost it! My entire hand was covered with blood.

Within seconds the blaring sounds of sirens moved closer. As traumatic as the situation was, I remember telling myself to calm down, and I did just that.

The EMT workers arrived and rushed into our apartment. They picked me up, placed me on the gurney and strapped me down. Crazy thing is, I never lost consciousness. I can still recall them talking over my head while transferring me to the hospital. I also remember them thinking I wouldn't make it. No one thought I'd survive.

Strangely enough, I didn't feel a bit of pain. I couldn't breathe nor feel my legs, but I was still coherent. I remember them asking my name and all the other important questions while in route to the hospital.

My mother and the rest of my family arrived twenty or thirty minutes later, fearing the worse. I was told that all four of the waiting rooms on the 5th floor of the hospital were filled with their hysteria. Emotions took many of them from prayer to retaliation. It was a chaotic scene, to say the least. I was in surgery for many grueling hours. I even flat lined twice.

Falling Into Your Purpose

After hours of surgery, they made the mistake of rolling my unconscious body past my family on the way to recovery. My head was slumped over and both of my arms were dangled on the sides of the gurney. Adding to that horrible vision was the fact that my entire body was covered with a white sheet. My sister later revealed to me that if she could've, she would've jumped out of the 5th floor window. The sight of my nearly dead body was just too much to handle.

Hours later the doctor walked into the waiting room and gave my family the news.

One single bullet shattered my liver, spleen, diaphragm, and my kidneys. That same bullet broke my spinal cord in half, collapsed both of my lungs and altered the course of my life. The good news was that I was alive. Although they weren't sure for how long, I was still alive.

After placing me in recovery they began allowing two family members at a time to visit me. One shift after the other, two by two, they each came in and passed out. The devastation was unbearable.

Day by day and week by week, they filled the waiting rooms with more love and support than I could've ever imagined. My will to survive was strong and my family's prayers were unending.

Two weeks later after stabilizing me, they did a fourteen-hour surgical procedure on my back. One month later they made plans to transfer me to The University of Ann Arbor where they were practicing stem cell transplants. The transfer would make it tougher for my family to visit, but they knew it was best for me.

After weeks of being in the hospital, I complained about the numbness in my legs. Every time I brought it up, I felt like I was being ignored. I sort of thought something wasn't right, but I assumed the high dosage of morphine was keeping my lower body numb so I didn't press the issue.

Two weeks before transferring me they decided to remove the tubes from my body. My dad and I watched the nurse carefully detached each tube one by one. After they all were removed the nurse adjusted my legs and then the sheets. Before she left the room I asked her a question.

"Why can't I feel my legs?"

She nonchalantly replied,

"Because you're paralyzed."

"**Paralyzed**?"

It was like the whole world just went on pause. Before I knew it I was screaming. And I mean that gut wrenching hopeless kind of screaming. I'm sure the sound of my voice echoed throughout the hallways of the hospital but I didn't care.

My father saw the initial look on my face as soon as the nurse released the word "paralyzed" from her mouth and he just walked out. He couldn't take it, and neither could I. It was the first time I'd thought it or heard anyone say it to me. Not once had the thought of me being paralyzed crossed my mind but it all made sense. That was the reason I was ignored every time I asked why I couldn't feel my legs.

Ironically, my mother was stepping off of the elevator at the exact time I heard the news. My screaming slapped her in the face the moment she stepped onto the floor. The devastation will forever ring in both of their ears. I don't think a word exists that describes how I really felt. My emotions were beyond measure.

Falling Into Your Purpose

After crying myself dry, I didn't speak for a couple of days. I just didn't understand any of it. I knew and had heard of people from my neighborhood that had been shot before. A few of them had experienced multiple gunshot wounds but every last one of them was still walking. Not one of their lives had been altered the way mine had been altered.

No matter how many times I went back and forth over it inside of my head, it just didn't add up. From here on out I'd be labeled as handicapped and would have to do everything from a wheelchair. It just didn't seem fair.

After almost two months and many surgeries later it was time for my transfer to University of Ann Arbor. My family wanted to lift my spirits before leaving so they invited my relatives and friends to the courtyard of the hospital for a going away gathering.

It was the most bittersweet moment I've ever had because it was the first time they had to put me in a wheelchair. There were at least one hundred people there for my send off. It was wonderful seeing them but sad to be in the state I was in. When they wheeled me outside, I saw all of them standing there looking at me with sympathy filled eyes. That moment broke my heart even more. I just couldn't believe they had to see me like that. 'How did I go from walking not even two months ago to being in this wheelchair? And when am I going to wake from this nightmare?' I kept waiting for the pinch, but the pinch never came.

The following day I was admitted to the U of M in Ann Arbor. My father insisted that they put me in a private room with a cot.

"I'm not going anywhere," he announced.

Sophia Janell Taylor

After the reality of being paralyzed sunk in, I became really evil. I didn't want to do anything and I didn't want to talk to anybody.

No matter what they did to pull me out of my stupor, nothing worked. The hospital even sent a paralyzed doctor in my room to give me an example of what life could be like after paralysis. I'll admit, I was amazed by him, but I remained evil and in denial.

Seeing the doctor in that wheelchair didn't take my anger away, but it did however give me an opportunity to ask him candid questions about his lifestyle.

No matter how inappropriate or embarrassing the questions were, he answered them all. He told me that he and his wife were expecting twins, and for that reason alone I was amazed.

"You still have sex?" I asked with no filter.

"Yes, I do," he replied.

My questions continued but offered no change in my position. There was nothing anyone could've told me or shown me that was going to make me want to live life in a wheelchair.

There are approximately 259,000 people in the U.S. living with spinal cord injuries.

The person that caught the brunt of my anger was my dad. I think I was so mean to him because he was the one there with me every day and there was nothing he or anyone could do to give me back what was now gone.

My emotions were all over the place. I just didn't understand why I'd been placed in this predicament. I was depressed and suicidal. All I wanted to do was lie in bed, but they made me get up and go to therapy every freaking morning at 6 a.m.

Falling Into Your Purpose

'Why so freaking early?' I used to wonder. 'And why am I in here cooking and folding clothes?'

"I'm a grown woman, I know how to do all of these things," I used to say. I now understand their tactics. They were trying to get me back into the groove of things. They wouldn't allow me to wallow in depression. They forced me out of it and back into the habits of life.

While in therapy, I met an eighteen-year-old quadriplegic named Kentrell. He was an extremely happy guy. Every morning he'd be sitting there smiling and I would be spilling over with agitation.

'Why the hell is he always smiling?' I wondered. I think his happiness aggravated me because I couldn't find anything to smile about.

One particular morning it was my turn to cook in class so I decided to make something really quick so I could get out of there and go back to my room. I threw some nachos together and the nurse fed them to Kentrell.

All of a sudden he started coughing and choking. He turned beet red like he was about to die. His convulsions scared me half to death and then I started crying. They began suctioning food out of him until he eventually calmed down. I just knew I'd killed him.

After the incident my dad started walking up the hall visiting Kentrell everyday. His family lived far away, so my father began looking after him like he was his own son. He couldn't really talk much unless the air was suctioned from his tube. I later joined in and began wheeling myself to his room for short visits.

One day I rolled myself down the hall and into his room. I pulled my chair up to the side of his bed and dropped my head on his legs. Within seconds I was sobbing. I mean really sobbing, and I couldn't stop. I just wanted to die. I gave in and let it all go. I didn't want to pretend that everything was alright, because it wasn't. Every regret and every emotion came rushing through and out of me.

It was all too much for me to accept. I felt overwhelmed with grief and pity. I cried so hard and felt so sorry for myself. I hated the fact that this had become my new life. I just didn't want to live like this and I didn't understand why I had to. Kentrell interrupted my pity party and gave me a reality check.

"I'd love to be in your predicament." Kentrell looked down on me after sucking air from his tube to speak.

"I can't even scratch my nose if I want to. At least you rolled yourself down the hall and into my room. Look at my shorts. They're bunched up on me like I've got on daisy dukes. Can you please straighten them out for me?" he said jokingly. It was kind of funny, but then again it wasn't.

That was the day I stopped feeling sorry for myself.

There I was crying after wheeling myself into his room, and there he was wishing he could've done what I was taking for granted. His predicament made me aware of how much worse mine could've been. That was the day I stopped feeling sorry for myself. He changed my outlook, which eventually changed my new life.

Outlook: A person's point of view or general attitude about life.

My family saw how lifeless I'd become. They were very concerned about my overall will to live. While I was in the hospital, my aunt was praying and searching for anybody that would breathe life back into me. One day she came upon an article in The Detroit Free Press entitled "Wheel to Survive." There was a picture of a man in a wheelchair below the title. She read it and immediately knew God had led her to it. The article featured a man that started an organization called Pioneers For Peace also known as P4P.

P4P would send people whose lives had been altered by guns into schools to speak to the youth about the effects of gun violence. The group would do speaking engagements all over the country. My aunt contacted him and within weeks he and a few people from the group were in my room at the hospital. They tried giving me encouraging words but I was a brick wall. I wasn't ready to receive anything they were saying. I still hadn't accepted the fact that I'd become one of them.

After almost two months of being in Ann Arbor I was released. The doctors and the staff had done all that they could do for me. Both hospitals had put me back together the best way they could. The rest was up to me.

I lived with my aunt the first two months after being released, then I moved back with my mom. The fact that she had to do so much for me was devastating. She had to bathe me, give me my medication and even cook for me. It was beyond humiliating.

It didn't take long for the visits and calls from friends to slow down. Loneliness and guilt settled in. I felt like such a burden. "If this is how my life is going to be then I don't want it." I made plans to end my life. All I needed was the right tool and the right time. I began plotting my escape from the world. "If they would just leave me alone around some pills or a sharp object I can put an end to this."

One day out of the clear blue my mother made an announcement.

"I think I'm gonna start sleeping with you."

"Sleeping with me. Why?"

"I just want to," she responded.

From then on, whenever night fell, my mother was right there in the bed with me.

I realize now that a mother's discernment is next to God's. She knew that if given the opportunity, I would have ended my life. I planned on taking every pill I could find the moment she left me alone. But God said no. My mother said no.

A mother understands what a child does not say.

One day the founder of Pioneers For Peace called me and said they had a speaking engagement in Flint and asked if I wanted to go. I initially said no, but I was bored and decided to go anyway.

Soon after, I was in the school's auditorium pouring my heart out to all of those kids. I hadn't planned on speaking but something inside of me pushed me up front. Before I knew it, I was talking to those kids from a genuine place of pain and concern, and they felt it. When I began speaking, I could see the lives that were being transformed by my story, and that's when the light switch turned on. That's when I realized what God was using me for.

What the enemy meant for evil God uses for good.
-Genesis 50:20

That day was like my awakening. For the first time since the incident had happened, I became aware of how my mother had been affected. She spoke to the kids about things I didn't know she felt. That was the day I realized that the incident didn't just handicap me, it handicapped us all. But it didn't break us.

Wear your tragedy like armor, not shackles.

I slowly began accepting my purpose. I joined Pioneers for Peace and began touring and speaking with them. We would go into the schools and talk candidly to the kids about their choices and the effects of gun violence. P4P consisted of 27 people that had been affected in one way or another by guns.

The guys in the group influenced me in so many ways. I watched how they moved about as if they weren't even handicapped. They were so fearless. They drove around without lifts on their cars and did things I didn't think was possible in a wheelchair. When my aunt bought me a van, I refused to get a lift installed. The guys in the group would bounce down steps and curbs like it was nothing, so I did the same. They would jet ski and do mostly everything else that folks with legs did. Their influence breathed life into me and made me fearless to a certain degree. Their spirit wasn't handicapped, so they moved as if they weren't. And I followed suit.

The only limits we have are the ones we put on ourselves.

I was in P4P for four years before tragedy struck again. The co-founder of P4P, Weusi Olusola had been diagnosed with bladder cancer. Within two months, the disease claimed his life. At 38 years old, he had changed more lives than most people with two feet ever would. He'd been shot by random gunfire at the age of 16. He was an All Star basketball player that later turned his misfortune into his purpose. He

Sophia Janell Taylor

resurrected himself and lived his life with passion and purpose. His influence inspired us all to do the same.

Weusi's death was such a devastating blow for us. Many of the members wanted to pick up what he'd taught us. He was so good at what he did. P4P ran like a fine oiled machine because of him. All we had to do was show up and speak. We had speaking engagements all over the country. We've done walks with Bill Cosby, jail tours and PSA's for the rapper TI. I've been on the Judge Hatchet show. We partnered with the Boys & Girls Clubs and spoke at all of the Job Corps in Detroit and Flint and many of the schools and colleges across Michigan. We would speak at 5 to 10 schools per week. We even played in the celebrity basketball games with the Detroit Pistons. We were also involved in the Million Mom Marches, the Saving Our Sons (SOS) movement, and we consistently did radio interviews.

We all had our own class in the summer at Capuchin Soup Kitchen for kids. The response we'd get whenever we'd speak was nothing short of phenomenal. The way some people described us was 'rock star' like. Those kids looked at us as if we were their heroes.

Since Weusi's passing, the group has split up. There are a few of us that still do speaking engagements. I still do them, because it's my passion and my purpose.

I'm proud to say that my testimonies have inspired so many people. I believe programs like Pioneers for Peace definitely help. One day I was speaking at Job Corp and a young lady stood up in front of all the kids and told her story of being raped and hog-tied by her older boyfriend. She was only 18 years old but filled with anger.

She'd been through more than I could ever imagine. She asked if she could come down and give me a hug. Through tears, she told me that hearing my story had completely turned her life around. Its kids like her that keep me going. They bless me in so many ways.

Show me a hero and I will show you a tragedy.
-F. Scott Fitzgerald

I believe those kids need to see somebody like them that speaks their language. Every time a kid shares their life with me, I get blessed. I think I'm so passionate about the lessons I give to them because I can see them. I can relate to them. It's like they're my life in the past, and we're their life, only fast forwarded if they don't take heed to our lessons.

I'm really raw and unfiltered when I speak. I admit the role that I played in what happened to me. I teach them to pay attention to signs and warnings. I encourage them to follow their elders' instructions and I tell them about the things I ignored before moving into that apartment. I let them know that they're not exempt from anything. It doesn't matter if you're black or white, right or wrong. What matters is following your intuition and warning signs, and more important is what you choose to do with them both. Heeding advice from elders and following your intuition are essential to survival. If my story can stop one person from going through what I've gone through, then my handicap won't be in vain.

Sharing has been my therapy and my way of giving back to the world. I always tell the kids that I believe things would've been different had I listened to advice and not rushed to be grown.

Listen to your inner voice and heed warnings.

I can admit now that before the incident happened, I was self-centered. Everything was always about me. Now I feel like my purpose is to influence and possibly deter others. If this had never happened to me my life would've still been all about me. Funny thing is I've always been told that I had an inner light. God knew the light he gave me would shine even brighter through my testimony.

I remember saying, "Why me?" I just didn't think I deserved this. I didn't drink. I didn't smoke. I was just trying to live my life. Weusi (the founder of P4P) used to respond to my question by saying, "Why not you? Nobody's excluded from anything."

To this date, the perpetrators of the crime have never been brought to justice. The detectives showed us pictures of the scene afterwards and it was unbelievable. There was blood splattered all over the walls and throughout the lower level of the apartment. There were at least fifty-seven empty shell casings from an AK47 outside of the building. There wasn't a window, a door, a wall or anything untouched. It literally looked like something out of an action thriller. Since the incident, the bricks on the outside of the building have been replaced. Unfortunately my legs will never be.

It's still hard to believe that we were victims of such a horrific crime. The pictures I saw were so surreal, but the fact that we survived the attack is more amazing. I know it was nothing but God that pulled me through. It wasn't the doctors. It was God. The doctors always told me that medically, I'm not supposed to be here. They told me that a man twice my size would've died instantly, obviously God had other plans for me.

Although I've adjusted to my new life, by no means has it been a walk in the park. I now live with half of a kidney. I have no spleen. My pain level stays between a 7 and a 10 daily and I've got so much metal in my back that it makes it impossible for me to lie in certain positions.

I haven't had a full night's sleep since the incident. I usually sleep 2 hours on and 2 hours off. When I'm in bed and having a really bad night, I push my upper body forward and lay my head on my thigh to try and sleep. It's a sight to see, but I do what I have to, to get a little rest.

I look at life now and realize the simple things we all take for granted. I never knew how blessed I was to be able to simply lie down in the position of my choice and go to sleep.

Although the incident happened years ago, there are still days I look over at my wheelchair and ask myself 'Is that mine?' There are days that I would rather crawl on cut glass than get in that wheelchair again. But I push through, and I move forward one more day.

Trust in the LORD with all your heart, and do not lean on your own understanding. In all your ways acknowledge him, and he will make straight your paths.
-Proverbs 3:5,6

In 2012, I finished school with a double major in social work and a minor in arts. Since the incident, I've moved to a different state and started a whole new life. My fiancé and I own Supreme Cutz Barber Shop and Supreme Refund Tax Service in Dallas, TX. I also work

Sophia Janell Taylor

for American Airlines as a reservation supervisor. Some say I do more than most people that have functioning legs. I say I move according to the spirit and will that God gave me.

"If you can't fly then run, if you can't run then walk, if you can't walk then crawl, but whatever you do you have to keep moving forward."

-Dr. Martin Luther King Jr.

I never knew the names of the perpetrators or what they looked like. I never wanted to know. I believe my family and I were able to move forward quicker because of the position I chose to take. I'm asked the same question time and time again:

"Don't you want closure?" What they don't understand is that I've got it. If I had dwelled on what happened to me, my family would have also. I wanted it to end with me. The bullets that shattered my life were meant for someone else, but they fell on me and I've accepted that. I could let it control my life, but I have a responsibility to myself and to my family to stay strong. I choose to focus on my future. I've chosen to release it and give it to God.

Beloved, never avenge yourselves, but leave it to the wrath of God, for it is written, "Vengeance is mine, I will repay, says the Lord."

Romans 12:19

I'm actually thankful that I don't have my assailant's faces creeping in my mind at night. I'm okay with the position I've chosen and I'm grateful that God has given me the kind of peace that could only come from him. I pray that their family never has to experience what mine have.

Falling Into Your Purpose

A key ingredient to happiness is being able to recover from adversity more quickly.

    My faith. My drive. My determination, and my family is what keep me going. I'm determined now more than ever to be happy, successful and helpful.
    I'll never let anything stop me from accomplishing my goals and my main goal is to be happy. Cars, clothes, money and material things don't matter to me. I just want to accomplish everything I ever saw myself doing, only from this wheelchair

Sophia Janell Taylor

My Survival Tips

1. Don't give up.

(There's always a light at the end of the tunnel.)

2. Don't' look at your situation as being a disadvantage.

(Focus on being the best you can be regardless of your situation.)

3. Understand that everything happens for a reason.

4. Find your purpose in what has happened to you instead of looking at everything as a problem.

5. Trust in God

I can do all things through him who strengthens me.
-Philippians 4:13

Falling Into Your Purpose

Purpose Pause

*The quickest way to change your life is to change your outlook.

*What the enemy means for evil God can use for good. Genesis 50:20

*Wear your tragedy like armor not shackles.

*The only limits we have are the ones we put on ourselves.

*Sharing is therapeutic and a way of giving back to the world.

> **Trust in the LORD with all your heart, and do not lean on your own understanding. In all your ways acknowledge him, and he will make straight your paths.**
> **-Proverbs 3:5,6**

Sophia Janell Taylor

TWO
LETTING GO

    I'm standing today because of the will and covering of God. I realize now that the greatest recoveries come after experiencing a great fall.

    For years I've been living my dreams and loving every mile of my journey. I'm a singer, a writer, an actress, a producer and a host. I'm also a real estate investor and an author. I know it sounds like a lot, but it's true.

    What kept the bills paid most of my years was real estate. I've been investing in properties every since I was 22 years old. My first house was purchased soon after I returned home from college.

    The newly refurbished house was located across the street from my parents. By my mothers' influence, without a job nor any real prospects of finding one, she convinced me to inquire about purchasing the house and consider becoming a homeowner early in life. Being that I was fresh from college, buying a home was the furthest thing from my mind. I just wanted to follow my dreams and float like many do at that age. Her nudging was relentless so I headed downtown to

Falling Into Your Purpose

find out the particulars. Much to my surprise the stipulations were unbelievable. The purchase price was only twenty four thousand dollars. The down payment was under one thousand and the monthly payments would start out at one hundred ninety three dollars with an (ARM) at 4% interest.

I could hardly believe the figures. I thought there was a trick to it, especially after returning home from living in one of the most expensive states in the country. You couldn't buy a garage for that price in Long Beach, CA., let alone a newly renovated house. I quickly got over my disbelief and signed the papers.

Meanwhile I had no job and no true plan of how I'd make the monthly payments. I figured at that price, I could collect bottles and pay for it every month. I was simply young and full of self- confidence.

Several weeks later I was approved for the house. I signed the papers and started my journey of home ownership and real estate investing. My heart and my drive gave me the courage to know that I'd be able to make the payments. At that price, I felt like I could swing two or three houses. It was then that I realized that the higher prices I'd been complaining about in California actually became one of the best things to ever happen to me.

Back in the day you could rent a four-bedroom house for three hundred and fifty dollars in Michigan. So going from those prices to paying nine fifty for a one-bedroom apartment was shattering to me. I compare living in California to muscle building. You never know how much you can lift until you try adding on more weight. That's when you realize your strength. Anyway, I signed my papers, received my keys and moved into my relatively new house.

Sophia Janell Taylor

At the age of 22, I was living in a four bedroom, two bathroom, two story home all by myself and loving it. While my friends were still living at home with their parents or still away at school, I bit the home ownership bullet early on in life. With no true nine to five, I managed to pay my mortgage and all the other bills that came with being a homeowner.

I've always had plenty of drive and belief in my passions so I turned one of them into a job. While living in California I involved myself in talent showcases, "extra" film work, and anything else that attracted me to the glitz and glam of the entertainment industry.

After returning home, I began promoting talent showcases and small concerts, which fed my creative thirst and put a little money in my pocket. This afforded me to make my mortgage payments. I soon began delving deeper into the arts by touring the country acting and singing. I've performed in many productions across the country and have been blessed enough to share stages with many renowned artists. My work kept me away from home constantly, but my bills were being paid.

One day an idea hit me to turn my house into an apartment. A simple adjustment, I figured. I found a contractor that could make my vision a reality. He threw up another entry door, converted one of the upstairs bedrooms into a kitchen and just like that, my owner occupied home was converted into an investment property. My parents and everyone thought I'd lost my mind when I told them my plans, but respected me for it later.

After the renovation, I continued performing and touring with the mental ease of having my mortgage

Falling Into Your Purpose

paid by the tenants below. Life was grand. Everything was falling in place until my mother received the diagnosis of colon cancer. Not having a nine to five gave me the freedom to go through every step with her, including traveling to a holistic therapy center in Mexico.

She was in the fourth stage of the disease when we arrived and was facing an uphill battle. She bravely faced her fears by going the alternative route. No radiation and no chemotherapy was how she chose to handle the situation. If only we'd arrived sooner. Maybe at an earlier stage of the disease she would've had a fighting chance.

After two months of being there, the doctors gave up, saying that they'd done all they could do. They predicted that she had less than two weeks to live and released her from the facility. I returned home before she did in order to prepare the house for her. There were so many things she couldn't have around her in the home and finding organic foods to aid in the process of cell rejuvenation seemed nearly impossible. We were all dedicated to fighting and winning this war regardless of their diagnosis. Perhaps I was in denial. I refused to accept their opinion.

It was close to the holidays when she and my dad returned home. Her strength and her fight were obviously fading. The day before Thanksgiving she was hospitalized again. One week later, she made her transition.

My mother's passing left us all empty and broken. Sorrow and depression began settling deep into my psyche. Every day I felt like I was stuck in a time warp or a cloudy maze. I couldn't escape it. I was so lost.

Sophia Janell Taylor

A few months later I decided to move out of my house and back across the street with my father. I placed an ad in the paper and soon after, rented out the top half of my home. I figured if both the upper and lower apartments were rented out, I'd have enough cash to move back to California to find myself. After my mother passed away, I literally felt like I was going to lose my mind. The only thing I could see myself doing was going far away and running on a beach.

One year later I was introduced to the concept of refinancing. I thought it was the best thing I'd ever heard of. I was so amazed that a house could do so many things. I pulled twelve thousand out of it and packed my bags. Refinancing felt like such a grown up thing to do. I planned to leave within the next week or so, but I wouldn't escape the city without following the whisper of another property.

This house was located two doors down from my boyfriend at the time. I hadn't had any intentions of buying another home. I had every intention of leaving town with my cash. I just wanted to live a little life. Isn't it funny how plans get altered!

One Saturday morning, my boyfriends' sister, mother and myself attended a bankruptcy auction. I tagged along out of sheer curiosity. I'd always wondered what went on in places like that. When we entered the room I was immediately sucked in by the energy. It was so exciting being there with all of those people.

They were like piranha's, trying to outbid one another. Listening to the man talk rapidly while describing houses heightened the electricity. I watched as people whispered to one another with hands from all sides of the room going up and down and up and down and I loved it.

Although I was only there as a spectator, I loved the excitement. Something about it made my insides jump. They auctioned off at least twenty houses and most of them appeared to be in good condition. I'd only tagged along to enjoy the experience but before I knew it my right hand flew up towards the ceiling then I heard the fast talking man say "sold to the young lady in the back." He was pointing and talking to me.

"What in the world did I just do?" I wondered. I'd just won the bid on a house that needed more work than I bargained for.

I knew owning another property would increase my monthly income but getting it together was going to prolong my move and I was ready to go.

With inspiration from my boyfriend's sister, we renovated the property ourselves. The experience was quite grueling, yet therapeutic. After completing the renovations, I found a tenant and soon after, headed back to California. I had no idea that I was turning into a real estate investor.

Not long after arriving back in California, I landed a gig touring again. Singing and acting on stage gave me enough money to rent an apartment. I even managed to save enough to go back home and buy another house.

Touring gave me the capital to pay my bills, invest and put a few dollars aside. Whenever I went back home I found myself eyeing other properties. My dad started telling me that I was addicted to buying houses.

Out of all the cities I've ever been to, I've never seen prices that compare to Flint, Michigan's. There were houses being sold from one thousand up into the hundreds of thousands of dollars.

On one of my many visits back home, I was introduced to a realtor named Bob. Bob started giving me property listings and advice. I soon found myself back in the renovation stages of another house and another house, and another. I was again reminded of the refinancing concept and you guessed it. I got deeper in the game of real estate investing. I refinanced one of my free and clear houses and purchased more houses.

With no true plan and no real knowledge of what I was doing, I'd become a real estate investor. I continued this process for a few years and found myself owning eleven houses in a very short period of time. I learned so much about purchasing, refinancing and renovating. When you're short on cash you learn how to get your hands dirty and do things yourself.

I've had my share of cuts, scrapes, and bruises dealing with those houses, but I honestly enjoyed every moment. I loved researching and touring properties. I enjoyed the way I felt after placing a bid on a house. I loved hearing Bob's voice on the other end of my phone announcing the great news that I'd been awarded a house that I boldly underbid on. It was such an exhilarating feeling.

I enjoyed shopping for material, laying carpet and ceramic tile. Hanging drywall and painting had become second nature for me. I found fulfillment in restoring those houses back into viable, habitable homes. I loved talking to potential buyers or renters and advising them on credit issues and housing choices. I honestly loved every aspect of what I had fallen into.

Falling Into Your Purpose

No matter what state I lived in, I found myself in Flint more than wherever I was actually living. I couldn't stay away. I was always there buying and renovating a house. I'll admit now that my lifestyle wreaked havoc on every relationship I was involved in. My passion for real estate was greater than my desire to settle down. There is no arguing that fact.

Eventually my travels took me to Atlanta, Georgia where I'd purchased a brand new condo in Buckhead, right in the heart of everything. My life had started to settle a bit. I was learning how to be happy again.

Whenever I'd return to Georgia from a Flint trip, I could do nothing but crash for weeks at a time. I would be so exhausted, but it was that good kind of exhaustion.

Our working careers will consume most of our lives, so we might as well do something we enjoy.

When I purchased my condo it was done with an ARM loan. This was only to get into the condo. I had a plan to refinance for a lower fixed rate in a year. The problem was, when it came time for me to refinance, the country was in the beginning phases of a recession. Everything would've run smoothly except for the fact that I'd signed for a loan for a business partner that disappeared and stopped making payments.

I've always been a stickler when it came to my credit. I prided myself on making the right moves with what I'd worked hard to get. I always made sure to pay my bills on time. I kept my debt-to-income ratio on point and my credit cards and their balances at a minimum. I could've kicked myself for allowing someone else to ruin it.

Sophia Janell Taylor

With the country's recession rearing its' ugly head and my credit score rapidly falling, everything I'd worked for was in jeopardy.

I quickly went into operation "save myself." I tried refinancing the condo, which in turn would lower my payment and the interest rate but with my business partner missing at least three months of payments, my credit score was plummeting.

Isn't it funny how you can pay your bills on time for years and years and it takes forever for your credit score to climb up. But, if you miss one payment your score will drop quicker than you can say the word drop. It's kind of like the Dow in a crash, but that's a whole other issue I have about our country's credit rating system.

Anthony's disappearing act sent red flags to my creditors, which made my attempts at refinancing my condo that much harder. Those three payments that he missed created a domino effect with all of my creditors. My available credit limits zeroed out. My purchasing power was shut down and my way of survival became threatened.

Anthony's disappearing act changed my life, but ultimately, my choice in allowing him to use what I'd worked so hard for did the most damage.

It seemed like in the blink of an eye, I crashed. It felt like overnight, life as I'd come to know it changed. I tried refinancing houses to save other houses. I tried negotiating with credit card companies to save things, but to no avail, my positive track record mattered none to them. Their only focus was the late payments.

Negotiating wasn't in their vocabulary. Everyone was thrown into a pool of non-negotiable terms during the recession.

Falling Into Your Purpose

Within a month, my condo's mortgage doubled and I was unable to refinance it for a lower rate. It didn't feel good, but I held myself accountable for every choice and every outcome that I made.

So there I was staring at bad credit, foreclosed properties, and a possible bankruptcy. This had become a nightmare and my new normal.

"What am I going to do?" I wondered to myself. I made some calls for a few jobs that never worked out. It seemed as if everywhere I looked jobs were being outsourced and people were being laid off. Companies were shutting down left and right. Salaries were being cut in half and families were being torn apart due to the economic crisis America was in.

"Maybe I should go back to school," I thought. Yeah, I'll go and get myself in more debt trying to get out of debt. That idea didn't sit well with me. Especially when I wasn't truly passionate about going back, and less enthusiastic about racking up more bills. I walked away from my condo and moved back to Michigan to regroup.

Sometimes you have to start back at one.

Once again, I was back with my father. I kicked some ideas around with him and of course he didn't feel good about the situation I'd gotten myself into. But he never once poured salt on my wounds. He watched and listened to my thought process about where I'd gone wrong.

My father is the person in my life that listens to me and supports my choices whether I succeed or fail. He's always been supportive of my free flowing nature. I'm sure it hasn't been easy having such a non-conventional daughter but he handles it all with a smile. He's been the ultimate blessing in my life. I couldn't ask for a better guide.

So there I was with bad credit, no job, one house remaining, and creditors coming after me for blood. Depression wanted to occupy my very existence. I tried my best to keep it out. "What am I going to do?" whispered in my ears constantly. I honestly didn't know what I was going to do. I couldn't see any good coming out of what was happening to me.

"Maybe I have lived haphazardly. I didn't create a parachute in case of failure. I hadn't planned for this." Those were the kinds of thoughts that haunted me for months. Eventually my depression and fear of the future turned into anger and drive to get back everything I had and more.

What I wanted more than anything was peace of mind. I didn't like the fear that I constantly felt. I felt so unappreciated when I tried negotiating with no negotiations on their behalf. I despised the constant phone calls I got from collectors. I hated wondering what I'd lose next and I vowed to never feel that way again. That kind of stress creates depression and anxiety.

I began being aware of my choices when it came to my feelings. I started evaluating my life like it was a movie and began changing the way I looked at it. That's when I started taking my power back. I grasped the fact that those corporations and creditors didn't care about me nor what I was going through. The fact that I was at home tossing, turning, and allowing them to stress me out bothered me more than anything. 'Wherever my creditors are, they're not at home thinking about me, so why am I allowing them to consume my every thought?' I mentally began turning them off.

Change: To make or become new.

My transition began when I changed how I felt about my situation. I started taking control of my emotions. I went from being reactive to proactive. I stopped concentrating on what I was losing and began looking at what I was gaining. Instead of focusing on the disease, I started concentrating on healing.

I could feel myself growing. Even though I was in the midst of the storm I began imagining myself feeling prosperous and free. I imagined my present situation as being in the past. I saw myself smiling and encouraging others with my story of how I made it through. I literally began looking at my 'now' as if it were my 'past.' I started accepting the fact that I may lose all that I'd worked hard for. Then I began looking at all I would gain by shedding those pounds of debt that were weighing me down. 'If I can let all these things go and walk away with some peace, I'll be free. Sure, I'll have to start over from scratch, but this time I'll be wiser.'

And be renewed in the spirit of your mind.
-Ephesians 4:23

I finally opened my tightly clenched fist and released what I was trying so hard to hold on to. I realize now that you can't receive anything new if you're holding on to everything from your past. My situation left me no choice. I had no more credit. I could only move about with cash, and that was basically zero.

Everyone in my close circle knew exactly what I was going through. They were all curious as to what I'd do next. They were looking for answers for themselves

Sophia Janell Taylor

because they too were caught in the middle of the economic crisis. They could offer me no resolve.

I counted my blessings when I saw how rough it was on everybody. Most of these people had families that depended on them to eat and keep a roof over their heads. Many had lost their jobs and their homes with little or no warning. It was so devastating.

Seeing this made me realize just how blessed I was. I didn't have time to waddle in depression. Being that close to so many people that were lost, inspired me to push myself and others that much harder.

I felt inspired to motivate and encourage everyone around me to turn their situation around. I had a 'stick it to the man' kind of drive.

'We'll show these corporations that haven't got a regret or an ounce of loyalty to faithful customers how resilient we are. We'll show them by pulling ourselves up by our bootstraps. We'll come together to help one another out of this mess.'

I became so proactive in my speeches and in my belief until I was almost neurotic. I was on fire with ideas and possibilities for tomorrow. I hated the situations that so many were in, but I loved how it made some come out fighting. I wished more would feel the power in themselves and realize that we all had given too much of it away.

The only way to encourage more people was to take the message to the masses and that's when I knew something great was about to come from my fall.

"A woman is like a tea bag; you never know how strong it is until it's in hot water. "
-Eleanor Roosevelt

We've all heard the old saying 'God doesn't make mistakes.' I believe this with all of my heart. The state

Falling Into Your Purpose

of our economy left many people depressed, homeless, stressed, hopeless and unsure of how they'd survive. I'm wise enough to know that not everyone was in this boat. There are so many people that benefitted from everyone else's grief. The abundant amount of foreclosures, job losses, school and job closing, etc., brought an opportunity for many that had the right mindset, cash, and credit. They became wealthy during our toughest time. This I'm sure of.

I've always felt that if I used my mind properly, I could pull myself out of anything and place myself in any situation I desired. I've always felt that if we would only realize the power of our minds and utilize it properly, we could turn any situation around.

I had a meeting with myself and began jotting down ideas from my journey as a real estate investor. My successes and failures on paper soon turned into a concept for a television show. I wanted the show to be candid in a way that hadn't been seen before. I envisioned the show being an inspirational tool for everyone. My hope was to inspire the viewers to dream, believe, and think outside the box. I wanted to ignite them to see the gem they're sitting on and reinvest in it.

I believed the things I'd gone through had given me plenty of knowledge to inspire some and warn others of the pitfalls and dangers of making wrong choices. I knew I had a niche for the lessons I wanted to give to anyone that would watch the show. I met my friend and videographer, Mike, and gave him the premise and the purpose of the show. Within weeks, my friend Andre and I were filming a reality show called 'Rehabin The Hood.'

Sophia Janell Taylor

One of the best sayings I've ever heard is, 'Life isn't about what happens to you. It's how you react to what happens.'

That statement is the epitome of truth for me.

"Success is not final, failure is not fatal: it is the courage to continue that counts."
-Winston S. Churchill

I began recreating myself by putting my energy towards helping others through the show. I turned my successes and failures into lessons. I didn't realize it but I was 'Falling Into My Purpose.'

I changed the way I looked at my circumstances and my circumstances began to change.

Falling Into Your Purpose

Rehabin' The Hood (RTH) has given me a purpose I hadn't seen coming. Yes, I lost mostly everything I'd attained. Yes, I became a bit depressed and hopeless. For a while, I was even unsure of myself and my future. When I changed the way I looked at my circumstances, my circumstances began turning around.

One day my father and I were sitting at the dining room table. He broke the silence by asking me a question.

"If you could do it all over again, what would you do different?"

I looked up at the ceiling and began reflecting on everything I'd gone through. I thought about the long lapse I went through without any money. I thought about the nights I tossed and turned, because my mind wouldn't shut up. I reflected on the times I begged for extensions from my creditors, and I even thought back on the properties that were seized behind it all. I looked over at him and responded.

"Nothing. I wouldn't change anything." I replied.

I No Longer Believe In Mistakes.

I now totally subscribe to the belief that everything happens for a reason. I no longer believe in mistakes.

I believe I'm where I'm supposed to be today and that I went through what I went through yesterday for a reason. Every choice I made and everything I've gone through has molded and shaped me to be who I am. With more wisdom and resilience than yesterday, I can truly say that my fall put me on the road to my purpose. Today I am happier than I've ever been. I'm stress and debt free. I've totally refocused my energy from making moves and money to finding ways to encourage others. I now see life through a different lens. In my eyes the glass is always half full. I now dwell in gratitude daily.

Gratitude is strongly correlated with optimism.

After experiencing the fall, as I've chosen to call it. I became so driven, focused and thankful. It was like something clicked inside of me. I felt like I had nothing to lose, so why not go after everything I want.

Some of the greatest businesses have started during a downturn or recession.

Today I'm a publisher and an author with several bestselling books under my belt. Rehabin' The Hood is aired all over the country. The show has educated so many people and created many amazing opportunities for myself and for others. I travel filming shows and performing songs from my cds.

I do live readings and signings for my books as well as motivational sharing all over the country. I host a television show called "Entertainment Spotlight" and I'm in production for a documentary, another cd, a few other film and television projects and I continue placing songs on other artists. I volunteer in my community and spend time with my family. And yes, I still find immense pleasure in turning a piece of property into a wonderful home.

When I share what I've gone through and show what came out of it all, people become inspired and encouraged to keep moving. I realize now that my mission in life is to inspire.

Had I folded during tough times, I would've never known what was on the other side. Those trials made me stronger, wiser and purpose filled.

Today I do things that bring my spirit joy. I don't stress about the workings of the world. I live everyday

Falling Into Your Purpose

giving thanks for being able to do what I love. I'm more grateful than I've ever been in my entire life.

I can't count how many times I say "I'm grateful" throughout my day. It's not that I'm trying to convince myself. It's just that I have an abundant amount of gratitude for the smallest to the biggest things in life.

I've created my own formula for living a happy life. I simply had to readjust what I gave energy to and reevaluate what truly makes me happy. Those simple adjustments allowed me to turn my fall into my purpose.

Peace is costly but it is worth the expense.
-A Kenyan Proverb

Sophia Janell Taylor

My Survival Tips:

1. Stay away from negativity i.e. People, thoughts, scenes, circumstances, i.e. (news, gossip, television shows, etc.) Surround yourself with positive uplifting people and experiences. Watch 'THE SECRET' it helped me tremendously.

2. Realize your worth. Meaning: your job or your finances should never define who you are.

3. Realize that most things are recoverable. Whatever you've lost in your 'fall,' unless it's a life, it can be reclaimed plus much more.

4. Change how you look at your situation! Instead of viewing your current 'fall' as a 'downfall.' View it as a blank canvas that's waiting on you to paint whatever you have inside of your mind. It's a new opportunity to search your soul and go after your true passion.

5. Don't think about 'them.' Don't place too much importance on people's opinions and man-made numbers, i.e. (credit scores,) (bank account balances,) (what people may say about you). Don't allow people or numbers to define who you are nor who you will be. Placing too much weight on these things will keep you ashamed, depressed and away from your purpose.

Falling Into Your Purpose

6. Listen to your inner voice.

Your inner voice will always direct you. Spend some me time getting reconnected to yourself and your higher being. Search and ask for guidance, regarding your future. Pray and Meditate, then try getting your mind off of yourself and your issues. Volunteering can bring great joy and a sense of gratefulness, which can also bring a whole new perspective to your situation.

7. Try something new.

Push yourself out of your comfort zone and your normal routine. Do something you wouldn't normally do. Incorporating daily walks may help. It did for me.

8. Believe in yourself.

When your pay gets cut drastically, don't waste more of your life being underpaid and unappreciated. Step out on faith and move out of your comfort zone. Ask yourself why everyone is using your gifts for their personal gain except you? Find and fall into 'Your Purpose.'

9. Losing everything could be your greatest gift.

You can't receive anything new if you're holding on to everything from your past. Let Go!

10. Envision the new 'You.'

Don't waste energy thinking about what you had nor your present circumstance, doing this will keep you stuck. Envision yourself being healthy, wealthy, happy and whole. Make it a purposeful practice every day to visualize who you want to be, what you'd like to do, or experience. Visualize your new life as frequent as possible.

A great practice is going to the bookstore and gathering magazines that interest you. Find a spot in the corner and flip through them all. This practice will help you visualize what you want. Whether its island living, a healthier body, an organization that feeds underprivileged children, purchasing cars for everyone, a new career, or painting pictures. This practice helps you to focus on what you want instead of what you don't want.

And the best part about it is that it's free....

So a man thinketh so he is...

Purpose Pause

*Sometimes you have to start back at one.

*Be proactive instead of reactive.

*Don't focus on the disease concentrate on healing.

*Look at your now as if it were in the past.

*Have a meeting with yourself and jot down ideas for a better future.

*Adjust what you give energy to and reevaluate what makes you happy.

*Recreate yourself by helping others.

*Change the way you look at your circumstances and your circumstances will begin to change.

*Recognize all the good things in your life and be spiritually and verbally grateful every day.

*And be renewed in the spirit of your mind.

Ephesians 4:23

Sophia Janell Taylor

THREE
CHOOSING YOU

The world will benefit greatly when you quiet your past and finally choose you.

I was born in Cook County Hospital in Chicago, Illinois. I grew up on the west side of the city. My mother had seven children. There were five boys and two girls. I am the youngest of the boys. I had a sister named Sharon that passed away at six months old before I was ever born. I had another sister named Genetra. Genetra and I were inseparable. Everywhere she was, I wanted to be.

My mother owned this beautiful mansion-styled three unit apartment complex on Chicago's Westside. Genetra rented out the basement, which kept her close enough for me to hang around her everyday. I'd often rush home from school and head straight downstairs to her apartment, just to be around her. I used to sit in her place watching television and eating up all of her food. I remember babysitting her five year old son while she made her runs.

We had a really close family. My mother and stepfather did their best at providing and keeping a handle on my brothers and I. We were definitely a handful. Nonetheless, we had a pretty good life.

The dynamics of our family changed the morning of June 21, 1976. It was two weeks to the date after my 8th grade graduation. It was around 2 a.m. We were all asleep when we heard someone beating at my mother's door. My sister's boyfriend was screaming and yelling at the top of his lungs saying that Genetra had just been shot. None of it seemed real. I just knew I was having a nightmare. How could it be when she lived right below us? We all prayed that it was some sort of joke.

We ran down to the basement apartment to see what happened with our own eyes and sure enough what he'd said was indeed true. I'll never forget seeing my sister lying on the bed with a bullet hole placed in the left side of her neck.

That vision will forever be engraved inside of my mind. I was only thirteen-years-old. Her son was five and Genetra had barely begun to live at the young age of twenty-one. I remember everybody going crazy trying to figure out what happened. My mom called the police while my sister's boyfriend tried giving us all the information he could. He told us what had taken place and who had taken my sister's life. At such a young age, I couldn't help wondering, 'Why aren't you dead also?' I felt like, if someone was there in the apartment with my sister, why hadn't her boyfriend fought to keep them off of her? Why hadn't he protected her with his life?

Sophia Janell Taylor

My sister was far from a push over. She was this feisty little chic, full of strength. I'm sure she did everything in her power to prevent the outcome. When Genetra was in the 8th grade, she'd thrown this guy through a chalkboard for grabbing her on her rear end. She was such a tough little cookie that grew up to be a confident, beautiful, independent young lady.

At the age of 21 she was all grown up and finding her way through the mean streets of Chicago. Come to find out, the same guy that caught a beat down from her in school started coming over to buy drugs from her. By the way, she was a drug dealer. We later found out that he stole her young life. We believe he set her up.

After my sister was murdered, the entire west side of Chicago was in turmoil. My brothers and I wreaked havoc on the entire neighborhood. Our anger was beyond control.

Genetra's death would be the turning point in all of our lives, especially mine. My pain turned into so much anger. My anger turned into this constant chip on my shoulder and the chip turned into mischief and violence, which inevitably grew into other things.

As a result of her death, many people lost their lives. My brothers and I belonged to a gang called the Vice Lords. We sold drugs and committed horrible crimes. We were young, angry and ready to lash out at the world.

At 15 years old I remember telling my mother she would never have to work again by the time I was 30. I vowed to be the biggest dope dealer there ever was. Her response was simply, 'Boy, you're crazy.' She fluffed me off as if I were talking sheer nonsense. My mother had a pretty good idea about what her children were doing out in the streets and she wasn't in support of it. I still hear her words like it was yesterday. 'If you ever go to jail, don't call me.' Needless to say, I never once called her.

My mother didn't encourage our activity, nor did she scream herself to death trying to stop us. She'd sometimes preach to us, yet still accept gifts at times from the money we made on the streets. I think she knew we'd eventually learn the hard way. On the other side, my step dad played no games. We knew he loved us and that he'd do anything for us. He was a good man and he taught me everything I know about home improvement. From plumbing, roofing, and electrical work, he passed all those lessons down to me and I graciously accepted them. I still utilize those skills today. Whether we were right or wrong, he protected us and stood by our side.

Before my sister was murdered, I began experimenting with drugs. I started smoking and selling marijuana at the young age of eleven from my sisters' downstairs apartment. I'll never forget being caught by my mother.

One day while sitting downstairs at Genetra's place, I heard a knock at the door. I assumed it was a customer coming to buy. I moved like a grown man answering the door with a joint hanging from the right side of my mouth. To my surprise, my mother was on the other side. I'd been busted and there was nothing I could do to escape. I stood there frozen. She snatched me up and threatened to beat the crap out of me if she ever caught me using drugs again. Sad to say, the drug usage continued, but the beating she promised never came.

Sophia Janell Taylor

More than 90% of harsh drug users began smoking, drinking or using other drugs before the age of 18.

Before my sisters' death, my mom's parenting style was pretty stern and direct. After she passed, it seemed like my mother turned soft or more passive than usual. I believe my sisters' death affected her in a way that we never quite understood. I know how it affected me and it didn't take long for me to show my pain to everyone.

My emotions were out of control. I became unruly and disrespectful in the streets. I was stealing, fighting, shooting, and selling drugs. I was the best thief I've ever known. I could steal a whole and leave the nail. That's how good I was.

The worst part was the elevation of drug usage. It got so out of hand at such a young age. I had done so many horrible things in my younger years but the one thing I never did was mouth off to my mother. That was a line I never crossed. A few years after my sisters' death, I began working for the Born Losers Motorcycle Club (B.L.M.C.) and that's when all hell broke loose. The club used to pay me two hundred dollars cash per week at the young age of 14, and that wasn't counting all the money I made from stealing from the gas station I worked at. I was turning a good profit at school from selling potato chips, soda, candy, etc. All of this came as a courtesy of the gas station, which was right next door to the B.L.M.C. They were both owned by the same folks.

As fate would have it I wound up attending the same school as the gang that was responsible for my sister's murder. Needless to say, there was a constant war going on between my crew and theirs.

Falling Into Your Purpose

    With all the drama in and around my neighborhood, I eventually dropped out my senior year of high school. Due to a direct result of my thievery, the school wouldn't allow me to come back. The sad part is, I was only one and a half credits' away from getting my high school diploma. I was so close to finishing but I gave up and gave in to the streets.
    The guys in the B.L.M.C. taught me how to ride motorcycles, and more importantly how to improve on my hustle. My duties were to pump gas and sweep up the shop, which I could handle with my eyes closed. When my mom found out how much I was making, she wanted me to start giving her one hundred dollars of my two hundred every week. I remember standing up to her as tall as I could with my chest poked out trying to negotiate with her.
    "I'll give you fifty a week," I said to her. She slapped me across the face and I still came back at her with the same price. I refused to budge on my counter offer. We reminisced on that moment years later and she told me that was the day she knew I'd be stronger than all my brothers because neither of them would've ever stood up to her the way that I had.
    With the money I was making at the gas station plus my side hustle cash, I began taking care of most of my own financial needs. I told my mom that I'd buy my own clothes. All she had to do was provide my shelter. I could handle the rest.
    Although I was making moves and becoming what the streets refer to as the man, I was still empty. The death of my sister left a big void in my life. I didn't care about anything anymore. What my family had gone through kept me angry. The anger I harbored made me want to hurt somebody. Anybody. The pain I felt was

so deep and nothing seemed to take it away. I was overwhelmed with grief and I just wanted to die.

I remember being told at a very young age that by the way I was living, I'd be dead by the age of 17. They were partially right, because I felt so dead and empty on the inside. I was a zombie walking the earth without feelings or a purpose. I was still alive but my will to live was gone.

Children that witness an assault on a parent or family member may suffer from Post Traumatic Stress Disorder, which can last well into adulthood.

My game soon elevated. I was selling and using cocaine and I didn't care about the consequences that could possibly follow. The vision of my sisters' lifeless body lying in that bed constantly haunted me. It took something away from me that I knew I'd never get back.

I'd never experienced death that close to me before, and it made me hate the world. As shameful as it feels to admit it, I even hated God. I didn't care about anything. I was on such a self-destructive path. I was an angry child that was turning into a cold hearted, hateful man.

Genetra would be the first of my siblings to get murdered. The second was my brother Deone. Deone and I were very close. As angry and hateful as I'd become after my sister's death, Deone's anger was one hundred times worse. He became a living nightmare. The anger my brother carried around steered his entire life. He was such a brilliant hellion.

Holding on to anger is like drinking poison and expecting the other person to die.
                                        -**Buddha**

Falling Into Your Purpose

When Deone was young, he was one of the smartest kids in our neighborhood. I remember hearing stories about how high his IQ was. It was said by people around us that he'd either be a genius or a damn fool. Unfortunately, the circumstances of our life turned him into the latter.

Regardless of the fear everyone else felt for him, I had nothing but love for him and I had no doubt that he felt the same for me. We would've given our lives for one another.

Just like the rest of us, Deone was a demon in the streets. If it was labeled wrong, Deone was going to do it. Out of all of us, he was the one you didn't wanna cross paths with. He took everything we were doing to a whole other level.

It was only a matter of time before he too would fall victim to the same streets that claimed my sister's life. There were so many people that wanted Deone to disappear off the face of the earth.

On March 7, 1990, their wishes were granted. Deone was found badly beaten with three bullets lodged in his head. He was only 32-years-old. I was 28 at the time of his murder.

His death opened wounds inside of me that had never truly healed. At that time, I had a wife and a brand new baby girl. I was doing well for myself but more importantly for the first time in a long time I was clean. It would only be a matter of time before my clean and sober lifestyle became a thing of the past.

Deone's death sent me spiraling downhill. The only difference between my sister's death and my brother's was the timing. This time around I was a grown man. I had access to more artillery, street connects and dope than I ever had before and I used them all just to numb my pain.

It didn't take much for me to pick up where I had left off. My self-destructive actions destroyed everything.

I lost my wife, my cars, my home, and the lifestyle I'd attained for myself. I was in so deep. I was doing terrible things to feed my anger and my drug habit. My addiction was so bad that I even began stealing from my own mother. I just didn't know how to stop. I didn't have a clue where to begin to stop.

"We cannot in a moment get rid of habits of a lifetime."
-Mahatma Gandhi

I knew nothing about sobriety or Narcotics Anonymous. I knew a little about Alcoholics Anonymous, but alcohol wasn't my issue. Drugs were my issue. I stayed out there doing what I knew to do.

My remedy for not facing reality was to stay high. As a direct result of selling and using drugs I began doing jail time by the age of 21.

I was the first of my mother's children to do prison time. What a title to hold! I would go in and come out, only to return. Jail had become such a revolving door in my life. I'd racked up felonies, a horrible drug habit, and three children. I had no high school diploma. No GED. No job. And I wasn't looking for one. I didn't know a company that would hire a man with a record like mine. Each time I got out, I'd find myself right back on that same old destructive path.

I survived in the streets by doing the same things over and over again. I've been busted for everything from aggravated assault to attempted murder. You name it, I've done it. I'd gone in and out of the prison systems and rehabilitation centers time and time again. I had no hope and no dreams. I honestly had no real desire to be on this earth. It's still hard to believe that I survived as long as I did. I was finally introduced to Narcotics Anonymous while serving a six and a half year prison sentence.

Scientific Research shows that addiction affects 23.2 million Americans. Only about 10 percent are receiving the treatment they need.

While incarcerated, I found myself being thrown in the hole so often due to my unruly behavior. I've been thrown out of so many prisons for being a danger to the staff and other inmates. The easiest way to deal with me was to keep me in solitary confinement. I believe I was there more than I was out.

Out of darkness comes light.

Who would've known that in my darkest, most hopeless hours, a glimmer of light would shine down on me.

Being in the hole is such a different experience. The utter and complete darkness, along with the total silence, puts you in a place of self-realization. At least that's what it started doing for me. My behavior kept me there. I soon found out that being in complete darkness and silence was the only way I would finally hear God speaking to me. That room created the perfect atmosphere for me to finally hear what God had been trying to tell me.

On April 26, 2000, I was released from the Illinois Department of Corrections Facility on the condition that I leave the state. I agreed and relocated. Some of my family members said when I left Illinois, the crime rate dropped at least 13.5%. How funny is that!

Sophia Janell Taylor

Soon after my release, I moved to Michigan. I was doing good when I first arrived, but like a record on repeat I started using again. I felt like my life was stuck on repeat. There I was in a new city doing the same thing. The drama, the jails and all the institutions seemed to follow me. I realized that the common denominator was me. I continued making the same choices until I became homeless, hopeless, and hungry in Michigan. Sounds like a television show doesn't it?

I was living like an animal and I'd finally hit rock bottom, but my bottom had a trap door. My choices were to lie down and die or get up and live. I finally made the choice to live.

Something clicked inside of me that made me want to experience a different life. I wanted to have fun and be around people. Getting high was no longer my definition of fun. I used to think it was cool and the social thing to do. If u didn't get high, you were square in my old book. Now I realize that my worst day clean is better than my best day getting high. I finally gave it to God and decided that I wanted to live. I no longer wanted to just exist. I finally came to the point where I wanted to experience the joy of living.

My last binge before giving it all up was a real hoot. I'd stolen money and bought lots of drugs and went on a smoking binge. This one was really bad. I don't think I could've gotten any higher. I began hallucinating and I even locked myself in the closet of the hotel and I wouldn't come out. It was in that closet that I began to pray. I asked God to take away my taste and my desire for drugs. I didn't want to feel that way ever again. I spent every dime I was making on drugs. I realized that I was on the losing end of this fight. I didn't have enough money to pay for another night in the room I was staying in. I'd reached my end and had finally gotten tired of being me.

After coming out of the closet and coming down off of being ridiculously high, I called my cousin to pay for my room for a few more nights. I gave her some story about how someone had done me wrong and how they owed me money. I put every ounce of sincerity in my voice hoping that she'd buy my story and come through for me one last time and that's when she let me have it. I wasn't fooling anyone but myself. She knew exactly what I had been doing. She'd been watching my dysfunctional cycle for way too long and she let me know exactly how she felt about it.

"You're too smart and gifted to throw your life away," she said to me. "Your mother is somewhere rolling over in her grave right now behind the decisions you continue to make. Stop playing the victim. Stop playing with me and stop playing yourself. Life is too short. Get your shit together before it's too late," she said before hanging the phone up in my face.

I had nowhere else to turn. I knew I'd be thrown out on my head the following morning. I remember praying really hard, asking with the most sincerity I've ever felt to be released from the demon that had such a strong hold on me.

The following morning, I walked down to the lobby knowing that they were going to tell me to get out but they surprised me by telling me that a young lady had come by and paid my rent for a couple of days. Once again, God had shown up and given me mercy and favor. But I knew that I couldn't keep living like that. I didn't want to anymore.

After those days that she paid for ran out, I voluntarily checked myself into rehab. There's a difference between being made to go and voluntarily going. For the first time in my life I became active and involved in the program. I truly wanted to experience the outcome of working the steps of sober living. I was totally dedicated to the transformation and renewal of me. I took it all in one day at a time. It's the only way it will ever work.

For I know the plans I have for you, declares the Lord, plans for welfare and not for evil, to give you a future and a hope. Then you will call upon me and come and pray to me, and I will hear you. You will seek me and find me, when you seek me with all your heart.
-Jeremiah 29:11:13

Today I realize that my life has a purpose. I'm supposed to help somebody become a better person. I'm happy to say that I worked the steps and so far the steps have worked for me.

I started a mentoring program called Inmate Mentoring Program (IMP). Imagine that, me a mentor. I feel so blessed to be able to speak to other young men and give them what I now have.

I'm honored beyond words to provide an open non- judgmental platform for these young men to talk about their past and the choices they've made following their experiences. We have heart to heart conversations about life. We talk about the triggers that caused them to choose the lifestyle they chose. We explore other options they can take to break the cycle. We laugh. We cry. We share. We shed. I let them know that if I can stop using drugs and find myself, and my purpose, then they can too. I'm not only helping the men that I mentor, but it does my heart good to be able to give back. It's been daily therapy for me as well.

Falling Into Your Purpose

Sheriff Chris Swanson and his staff gave me the opportunity of a lifetime by allowing me to go into the jail system and be a beacon of light to others that are living the same lifestyle I once lived.

I've finally become a well-rounded person with a desire to move outside of myself and help others. I now feel that I have a voice. That voice comes from first hand experiences which gives me the knowledge and the empathy to relate to those going through what I've been through.

Those men see and feel the sincerity and passion I have for helping others who find themselves caught up in the madness.

I'm wise enough to know that there will always be triggers in life that try to take me back to that lifestyle, but I stand strong in my purpose and my belief in knowing that it's God who keeps me and provides all of my needs.

I cry out to God Most High, to God who fulfills his purpose for me.
-Psalm 57:2

In 2013 my oldest son suddenly passed away. It was the most devastating thing I've ever experienced. I can still hear his voice the day we reunited a few years prior to his passing. Regardless of the devastation, I'm grateful we had the opportunity to reunite. I know he's with the rest of my family and they're all watching over me now. Through it all, I've been blessed with another chance at life.

I'm grateful for the opportunity to be reunited with all three of my children and hear their voices call me 'Daddy.' I couldn't ask for a better gift than that.

Sophia Janell Taylor

Each day I ask God to allow me to be a blessing to someone else. It's not all about me anymore and now I realize that it never was.

My hope for IMP is to continue helping inmates of both sexes and all races. I want to encourage them to become productive members of society. I want to continue offering as much assistance as I possibly can, whether it be helping them find housing, becoming active members of their family or encouraging them to take steps to become employable. My mission is to love on them and help them realize that they are not a lost cause. As long as you have breath in your body, you can make a different choice and start again.

Today I look in the mirror and not on the mirror.

It took me a minute to get here but I can honestly say that I love myself. Today I look in the mirror and not on the mirror and I like what I see. I'm no longer hungry hopeless or broke and I thank God. The guy that used to be behind those cells now volunteers his time conducting meetings in hopes of changing a life. I walk through the jail hallways on a mission to give hope and guidance to those that need it. Today I'm happy, fulfilled, and a productive member of society.

My present peace comes from praying and meditating on a daily basis. I now earn an honest living driving trucks and doing home repairs. More importantly I give back to the community that I once tried to destroy.

On August 25, 2016, I celebrated 10 years clean and sober. I am a miracle. Of all the people in my life that tried encouraging me, there was one person that finally got through to me. And she is the creator of this book. She showed me unconditional love, even in the

Falling Into Your Purpose

midst of my madness. Many people said things to get me to change my behavior, but for some reason her voice was the one I heard. She was my angel. We all have one. I think more than anything, I'd reached the point where I was ready to listen.

Addiction can be effectively prevented, treated and managed by healthcare professionals in combination with family or peer support.

I realize just how blessed I am to be in this place at this time of my life. I truly believe that God has spared my life for a reason. My service work has confirmed to me that falling over and over has a bigger purpose, especially when you finally get up. It's all for a purpose bigger than we can see.

He will wipe away every tear from their eyes, and death shall be no more, neither shall there be mourning, nor crying, nor pain anymore, for the former things have passed away."
-Revelation 21:4

Sophia Janell Taylor

My Survival Tips

1. No matter what happens, just don't use!

2. Don't concern yourself with who may know about your past, as long as you don't forget it!

3. 'I' can't, but 'We' can! (Surround yourself with positive, like-minded people.)

4. When you find yourself in a hole. Stop digging.

5. Know that you have to go through everything you've gone through, to become the person you are meant to be.

*There will come a point in life when you have to make a choice. Do something different and you'll get a different result.

Purpose Pause

*Work the steps and the steps will work for you.

*Ask God to allow you to be a blessing in someone else's life.

*Realize that your journey is not about you and that it never has been.

*As long as you have breath in your body you have an opportunity to start again.

*Pray and meditate daily.

*Realize that everything happen for a bigger purpose than our eyes can see.

*Do something different and you'll get a different result.

Sophia Janell Taylor

FOUR
PLAYING THE HAND I WAS DEALT

 The makings of being a wonderful life formed well before I was in my mothers' womb. My mother was beautiful smart and gifted. My father was really handsome with a great amount of talent to match and they both came from really good families.
 Fate seems to have a way of positioning people to fit in its' plan. My parents grew up one block from one another. Their love for the arts became another thing they had in common. The stars aligned, they became a couple and well, here I am. Unfortunately commonalities weren't enough to keep the young couple together.
 I was in elementary school when they split up. Like stories flow they both carried on and wrote new chapters to their lives. My father married and started another family. My mother did the same. I was still in elementary school when my mother married my step dad. He was a nice guy. I remember how he would chase me around the house while I giggled non-stop, running and screaming. He and I would hide from one another, then, discover where the hiding place was,

yelling out "I found you!" Those are really good memories.

I was such a frail little girl. I remember how he'd pick me up with ease, holding me over his head or throwing me around tickling me until I could take no more. He was a fun guy. Of course I'd rather experience moments like that with my own father, but I took what I could get. When you get down to it, all a kid really wants is to be shown attention. They wanna feel safe and loved. It's always a plus when those things come from the parents.

Adding to my stepfather's brownie points was the fact that whenever I'd get in hot water with my mother he would stop her from spanking me. If my mother said no to something that I wanted, he'd step in and play the good cop role, convincing her to let me have whatever it was that pleased me at the time.

It took a minute for me to adjust to seeing my parents with other people. Although I was only a kid, I didn't like them being apart but I adjusted and played the hand that I was dealt.

Not long into the marriage my mother became pregnant with my brother. From the moment he arrived, I absolutely adored him. I wanted to do everything for him. I used to beg to feed and change him, and I always wanted to hold him. He was so tiny and adorable. There was nothing I wouldn't do for him.

One day my step dad and I were running through the house playing. My mother wasn't home at the time. Not that it mattered, because we would play the same way when she was there.

This particular day I was down for the count. I'd once again given in to laughter while he hovered over me with dancing fingers prodding at my funny parts.

Sophia Janell Taylor

One of his favorite things he liked to do while playing with me was placing his lips to my stomach, acting as if he were blowing bubbles on my tummy. It's usually done to toddlers but nevertheless I'd laugh as if I were smaller. I never thought anything of it until the day discomfort followed my laughter. That was the day the layers of my innocence began peeling away.

I believe I was in the 5th grade when the playing took a sharp left turn. I'd grown used to laughing and running through the house from him. On this particular day, I had on these 'onesies like' pajamas. We were running around playing, as usual. He held me down making me laugh then in mid tickle he unbuttoned my pajamas and began nuzzling his head down onto my stomach acting as if he were blowing bubbles.

He moved his head further south then pulled my pajamas over to the side and placed his mouth on my private parts. I was startled. I didn't know what to do nor what had just happened. He made sure to do it really quick then he hurried up and put me back the way I was. He quickly flipped the switch acting as if nothing had happened.

"Come on, let's go in the other room," he said trying to return the mood back to normal. It was confusing and I remember feeling really weird.

His inappropriate advance gave me this strange sensation. I didn't really have the vocabulary or the knowledge to describe it or know what he had done. I just knew I felt uncomfortable.

Unfortunately, as time moved on those feelings and the encounters continued.

A child molester is any older child or adult who touches a child for his or her own satisfaction.

Falling Into Your Purpose

I now understand that if left unchecked, a pedophile's ego will command them to carry out their fantasies. Neither age, circumstances, risk nor relation matters when it comes to their illness. Perhaps these are the reasons he was capable of going further and further each time.

His boldness progressed along with late night visits to my room. It was usually done in the name of 'tucking me in.' His advances and requests grew and soon became protocol. The dysfunction quickly morphed into reciprocation.

He showed me how to clean him and myself properly before performing oral acts. It wasn't until he made me have my first orgasm that the feelings of guilt and shame hit me. That's also when he instructed me not to tell anyone. It was so confusing to my young mind. I remember covering my face with the pillow every time he'd act out his fantasy. I felt like I was doing something bad and that I would get in trouble if anyone else knew, especially after he'd manipulated me into silence.

"You don't want your brother to be without a father, do you? If you tell they'll take me away and then your brother won't have a dad anymore," he said in hopes of silencing me.

Knowing how I felt about my brother, I honored his request. I would give my life for my brother and he knew it. There was no higher manipulating tool he could've used.

At 10 years old he'd escalated my physical and emotional femininity, and at the same time he imprisoned me mentally.

Sophia Janell Taylor

Forty-four percent of sexual assault victims are under the age of 18, and one in 10 children are abused before the age of 18.

The act of having an orgasm made me feel horribly confused. Each time I'd cover my face with the pillow while my body responded. Each and every time my mind would be riddled with guilt. The routine eventually became protocol. Night would fall, I'd wash up and get into my bed and soon he'd enter. There were no questions asked. I'd just lie on my back and grab my pillow in preparation for the routine.

At such a young age I became addicted to the feeling. Many people don't understand what sexual abuse is. It's really sexual seduction. You're seducing a child. You're doing something to a child's mind that they eventually learn to like. Their body responds to it and they get addicted to the pleasure part of it. It's human nature.

And that's exactly what happened. I unwillingly became addicted to the attention and the feelings that I experienced. I was trapped inside of my own home. The enemy lived with me. He played with me and tucked me in at night. He was the husband to my mother and the father to my brother. He was the gatekeeper.

89% of child sexual assault cases involve persons known to the child, such as a caretaker or family acquaintance.

That scared little voice inside of me told me that I had no other choice. I had to go along with everything he tried because I would be in trouble if anyone else knew my secret. If I told, my brother wouldn't have a father anymore. Both burden and guilt weighed on me daily. I became really quiet and secluded in school. I remember sitting in class looking at all the other kids, wondering if every girl was going through what I was going through. I wondered if this was a normal life. I had no idea how horrible of an act it was because I had nothing to compare my life to. I kept it all to myself.

A child who is the victim of prolonged sexual abuse usually develops low self-esteem, a feeling of worthlessness and an abnormal or distorted view of sex. The child may become withdrawn and mistrustful of adults, and can become suicidal.

From the age of ten up until I was fifteen years old I was sexually molested, mentally manipulated, and socially inept. My only escape during the later years of the abuse was my artistry. By my real fathers influence I became heavily involved in dance. I was phenomenal at tapping and singing as well. It became the thing that took my mind where I wanted to go. Away.

I moved robotically throughout my days at home. The routine had become just that. A routine. He'd acclimated me into a life that required silent willingness. Whether my mother was at home or away he did as he pleased, entering my room, manipulating my body and confusing my young mind.

Through the years of exchanging oral sex he never entered me vaginally. I don't believe he refrained out of kindness. I think he was being smart. He knew if I ever told, the first thing the doctors would do is check to see if my hymen had been penetrated.

When I got into my teens, my body's urges for what he'd acclimated me to, grew. There would be nights when he wouldn't come into my room. Those were the empty nights. Like a spirit rising up and hovering over me, the cravings would take a hold of me. I missed the release. I had become addicted to the dysfunctional routine. I was so young mentally, but I had the experiences of a grown woman. I went from being shocked and confused to feeling guilty and ashamed, to accepting, craving and anticipating. This is what my life had turned into.

At fifteen years old, I finally found the courage to break my silence. I remember sitting in the living room watching an episode of Highway to Heaven. On this particular episode, a girl had been gang rapped and for some reason watching it triggered something inside of me. Next thing I knew I was crying and I couldn't stop. There was a voice that came to me saying, "It's time. You should tell her. Tell her." It repeated. The voice convinced me to take that long walk to my mothers' bedroom. It seemed like the longest walk of my life. My sobbing grew with every step I took. I entered her room and climbed into her bed crying like someone had beaten me. I just couldn't stop crying.

"What's wrong?" My mother asked, but I couldn't get any words out.

"What happened, is it a boy at school?" I continued crying.

"Has your step father done something to you?"

I shook my head up and down which made me cry even harder.

"What did he do? Tell me," she asked.

My crying had reached its' peak and my shoulders were hunching uncontrollably, then suddenly I became overwhelmed with exhaustion. All I wanted to do was sleep.

"I just wanna go to sleep," I said through my sobbing.

Falling Into Your Purpose

"Can I just go to bed? I just wanna go to sleep," I said as I walked back to my room and climbed in my bed. Seconds later I was out like a light.

That was the best sleep I've ever had in my entire life. I guess my up and down headshaking was enough to relieve the pressure of the world from my young mind. Finally the weight had been lifted.

Most victims never tell because their ashamed or protecting other family members.

My confession came during one of their many splits. At that point he would come and go but the relationship had ran its' course with her also.

After that day I never saw him again, but the damage had been done. The guilt, shame and all the other seeds of negative emotions had been planted. They began to sprout and grow in the wrong direction.

When it all came out, I felt relieved. My family wanted me to go to counseling but I wanted to be left alone. They wanted me to testify and tell the courts what he'd been doing to me but I wasn't open for it. It was all too stressful and draining. I felt like I'd done enough and gone through enough. I just wanted to live a normal life.

Like rape, child molestation is one of the most underreported crimes: only 1-10% are disclosed.
-FBI law enforcement

When I was in the tenth grade I began experimenting with marijuana. It helped me feel free and outgoing and it became my escape from reality and responsibilities.

I realized when I started dating that many of my "first times" had been taken by him. I pushed through the flashes of my life that came whenever I was out being a teenager. My boyfriend and I would be out

Sophia Janell Taylor

smoking and fooling around, but the haunting of my home life stopped me from actually having sex. My girlfriends use to tease me, calling me a square for not going all the way but they had no clue what I was going through at home.

As time progressed, I became more involved in my art. Dancing and singing gave me a bright side to a dark situation. They brought me out of my shell. I was finally getting attention because of my gifts and it felt good.

By the age of sixteen my skills grew along with the smoking and dependency for emotional support. I didn't know what to do with what had been done to me. All I could do was dance, breath, and sing.

Before leaving for college, I began experimenting with weed laced with crack cocaine. I didn't see it being a problem. I was functioning and getting through life like everyone else.

My gifts took me to North Hollywood, California where I was awarded a scholarship for dance at the Tremaine Dance Center. It was so exciting to be rewarded for doing what I loved to do. I looked forward to my new beginning.

For years I struggled with feelings of loneliness, and being that far away from home didn't help. It didn't take long for me to fill the void and get involved in a relationship. My focus shifted and soon I became off balanced. I frequently got caught up in emotional booby traps.

My drug usage escalated and that's when I realized I had an addiction. I returned home and spiraled further downhill.

Victims of prolonged sexual abuse often develop low self-esteem, a feeling of worthlessness

and an abnormal or distorted view of sex. The child may become withdrawn and mistrustful of adults, and can become suicidal.

My family sent me to a rehabilitation center. I was there for a few months. I left there and started using again. Every time I used, I would spiral down even further. My life had become a record with loads of scratches. I was stuck on repeat.

The National Institute on Drug Abuse (NIDA) reports that the relapse rate for drug addiction is 40 to 60 percent.

I moved to upstate New York and enrolled in school. I was only smoking weed at the time, but it didn't take long for me to slide downhill again. Each time I went to counseling, they would tell me that I needed to deal with being molested. I needed to deal with my past. I just didn't get it. I thought I was dealing with it. I didn't really understand what they meant. I figured if I wasn't having flashbacks when I was with a man then I was okay. I understand now what they meant by dealing with it. Thank God I finally get it now.

Research has shown that it takes anywhere from two to eight months to build a new behavior or pattern. You'll never find out if you don't start at One.

I had to learn a lot about the disease of addiction. After many times of attempting sober living, I understand now what I didn't. The important part of it all is that I never stopped trying.

It took me six years of trying to get to twelve years of continuous sobriety. I've gotten through the years by living life one day at a time.

Sophia Janell Taylor

Every accomplishment starts with the decision to try.

In celebration and support of myself and other survivors of child molestation, I formed a foundation called "I Found My Voice." It's a performance-based project that helps survivors of domestic and sexual violence heal. It's done every year and it involves people from all walks of life working for a common goal. That goal is prevention and healing.

My artistic background drives the vision and paints pictures that spark communication and understanding. Every year people from across the globe come and present their stories in their own unique way. Each year the venue is packed.

My family lends their gifts and support to the cause by painting, dancing, singing, styling, choreographing and assisting. Others express themselves through dance or poetry, while the band accommodates them.

I am beyond grateful for them all. It's been a labor of love for me to be able to pour my emotions into this project. We provide workshops and counseling the entire week leading up to the event. We laugh, we cry, and we heal.

"I Found My Voice" has given me a platform to present my gifts in a light that's pleasing to my soul. I'm able to inspire others through my story and my talents while saving my own life in the process.

They overcame him by the blood of the lamb and by the way of their testimony.
                                                -**Revelations 12:11**

The first year of "I Found My Voice", I was terrified. I stood on that stage and shared my story in front of hundreds of people. I kept it raw and unfiltered. I wasn't sure what kind of response I'd get. I just did what was on my heart. At the end of the show everyone was on their feet applauding and many were even crying. It's the best feeling when people come up to me and express how I've enhanced their life. It's one of the greatest rewards to receive.

Who knew that my life and my vision would create such a response. I never knew how powerful speaking out could be.

Sharing your story can help others become strong adult protectors of the children closest to them.

I'm grateful for everyone that selflessly gives their time and gifts to the project. I'm grateful for my family that supports my vision and my efforts, and I feel blessed to have the community encourage and support my vision.

Recovery is designed to be a bridge back to life. But this has been my bridge back to the stage.

I'm working towards taking the show on the road. My ultimate goal for "I Found My Voice" is Broadway. I believe projects like these help to heal, educate and deter wrong behavior. I just want to touch people and do my part to bring awareness. And I want to inspire others to do the same. I've become a teacher and I believe that "I Found My Voice" is putting me back in a place where I have drive and focus. It's given me a zest for life. There are some things that have happened in my life that have robbed me of that, and I just want to get it back.

If I had to choose my life all over again, of course I wouldn't choose the one I was handed. Nobody would choose the life I endured, but I'm playing the hand I was dealt and making the best of it.

Sophia Janell Taylor

I understand now that parenting is a trial and error journey. I truly believe if my parents could go back in time, they'd make different choices. At this point, the only thing I can do is forgive myself and all parties involved. I can't allow my past to imprison my future.

Every struggle in your life has shaped you into the person you are today.

I'm still figuring things out, even today. I realize I will always need help, but I take it one day at a time and I do my best to stay in a grateful space.

There's a saying in recovery that I've adopted: "There is no catching up, just catching on."

My goal now is to have complete emotional and spiritual freedom. I'm finally learning about myself on a deeper level. I understand now that I have to stay in a process of learning and self-discovery. It helps me to survive my emotions. The memories from your past may never completely go away, you just learn how to survive the emotions.

You don't realize your own strength until you come face to face with your greatest weakness.

My Survival Tips

1. Connect with other survivors

(It gave me hope and let me know that I wasn't the only one.)

2. Connect to something creative outside of work. (i.e. gardening, painting, writing, etc. prayer/ meditation)

3. Find one person that you can tell the absolute truth to and have the truth told back to you.

4. Never stop self-discovery. (Realize that the healing process is lifelong)

5. Always remain teachable.

> **I call on the Lord in my distress, and he answers me.**
> **-Psalm 120:1**

Sophia Janell Taylor

PURPOSE PAUSE

*It's not what happens to you, it's what you do with what happens to you!

*Your best teacher is your last mistake.

*Every accomplishment starts with the decision to try!

*There is no catching up, just catching on!

*Never stop trying.

Falling Into Your Purpose

In order to break the chains from your past you've got to learn to accept yourself. That includes your flaws, and even the choices you made during difficult times in your life. We all have an opportunity to grow after making choices that we're not proud of. The blessing of life is that you can share your experiences with the next person in hopes of steering them in the right direction. Remember, you made it through for a reason. Your ability to survive is a part of your purpose.

Sophia Janell Taylor

FIVE
SEARCHING FOR ANSWERS

    The gavel hit the wooden block and my knees went weak. Twenty-two years and no more than fifty is what they sentenced me to. Flashes from my short life play before my eyes as I stood there listening to the judge's voice echo then slowly disappear. The room seemed to spin and suddenly go on mute. The sounds from my family's cries pierced through the silence and landed on my heart. That's what hurt the most. It was the sobbing from the heartbroken families that tore me apart. For that reason alone perhaps I would've made a different choice.
    Unfortunately clocks don't rewind. What was done was done. The sheriffs ushered my shackled body out of the court room and into a whole new world of grief. I was a kid about to make the transition into manhood behind the bars of the system.
    My first week of incarceration gave me plenty of time to think about the choice I made, and I regretted it all. I regretted taking vengeance into my own hands. I regretted the heartache I put his loved ones through and I hated the fact that I had disappointed my own

family by dragging them down this road with me. "If only I had left it alone." I often thought to myself. "If I would've just let God handle it, I'd be at home doing what most teenagers were doing. Living life! If only I had listened to my grandmother."

I was the kind of kid that always wondered about things. I was always so full of questions. I used to wonder why my mother would leave me in empty rooms at strange men's houses while she disappeared behind closed doors. My little forehead would wrinkle in wonderment whenever I heard the strange noises coming from the room they were in. I wondered why I lived with my grandparents. And why did some people's lives seem better than others?

From the backseat of a police car, the entire hour long trip I wondered where my mother was as they delivered me to my grandparent's house.

"Why is my grandmother the only one here for my parent teacher conference? Where is my father and more importantly, who is he?" I wondered all of these things.

Some kids are born with luxuries that they take for granted. Then there are those kids like me that wished they could be them. Why couldn't my life be like Theo's from the Cosby Show or Peter from the Brady Bunch? Their problems were so minute compared to mine.

The sting of life's bitterness filled my lungs on September 5, 1973. I entered this world with the burden of so many unanswered questions.

During dinner one rainy evening, my mother stood and made the announcement that she was pregnant. At the young age of fourteen her confession sent them all reeling, provoking a lightweight hysteria. They demanded to know how, when, where, and by who?

Sophia Janell Taylor

She gave them what they wanted, which was answers. They may not have been truthful ones, but her young mind gave them what she thought they could handle at the time.

From inception, my life had been a load of questions. Perhaps I've made it this far simply to find the answers to them all.

Insecurities, fears and frustrations spilled over from my mother's life and into mine. As a young boy I remember moving about in search of something. I didn't always know what I was looking for. I just knew something was missing.

On the outside my mother was living the same way I was feeling on the inside. Reckless.

My grandparents would turn out to be both of our saving graces. They did their best to fill our voids, but there was only so much they could do. I guess we both had to meet the wall head first before turning it all around.

I came up in a neighborhood full of love, but it lacked in connectivity. The missing piece was the fathers. More often than not, it was the mothers, grandmothers, and aunts that reared the neighborhood children.

Don't get me wrong. They did the best they knew to do. As hard as they tried, they could never be what little boys hungered and cried for. A woman can never fill a void that a man leaves behind. Little boys go through life looking for that missing piece to their puzzle. They may never admit it, but until the day they die, boys will always desire a man to guide, protect, and love them.

My example of manhood came from my grandfather. He worked hard, provided for his family and went above and beyond the call of duty. He took on the responsibility of caring for my little brother and I. We could've wound up separated and in foster care but my grandparents done what they could to keep us together. They tried their best to give us what we were missing.

We never went without a meal, a roof over our heads or clothes on our backs as long as we were with them. But that still didn't stop me from wondering about life or desiring something different.

In order to survive in my neighborhood, you had to have guts. Guts to walk through the streets, to run with certain clicks, and you had to have guts to do what you had to do in order to survive.

There came a point in my life where I wanted more than what my grandparents were offering. That's the point many teenagers in urban areas come to. That call from the streets ring and the neediest kids eagerly answer. It's the excitement and the perks that come with the territory. It's the connection to like-minded kids that have the same feelings of void as you do. It's the brotherhood and the fast come up. Simply put, it's life in the hood.

Around the age of eleven or twelve, I turned my street hustle on and my school attendance off. School just wasn't important to me. I used to walk in the front door and right out the back. I missed so many days until there was no sense in me wasting the teachers' time. So, I just stopped going.

It's funny how things seem to magically appear when you're searching for them. I knew I wanted more of something, I didn't quite know how to get it.

I caught the bug for life in the fast lane one summer while staying with some family members in

Sophia Janell Taylor

Detroit. My young mind watched my cousins' older friends make street transactions and live a life that seemed just as exciting as it looked in the movies. The beat from the trunks of the Jeep Cherokees filled me with more excitement than I'd ever felt. The rims, the shiny paint jobs, the motorcycles and their flashy clothes all made a desire for a better, faster life, grow inside of my young mind.

The way they'd flash big wads of money and the women that came with their lifestyle had me salivating. I was sold. I wanted in. I needed some of that, and there was nothing I wouldn't do to make it happen.

I returned home at the end of the summer with one goal in mind. I'd decided to become the biggest drug dealer anyone had ever seen.

My grandfather's decline to purchase a mini bike I'd asked him for sealed the deal to my financial emancipation. True enough, my grades were less than favorable, and my attendance was subpar to say the least. But I saw no reason for him to decline my request for something I wanted so badly. His "no" pushed me to go from begging to making it happen myself.

Do not be anxious about anything.
-Philippians 4:6-7

When you live in the hood, you don't have to look hard to get into a life of street distribution. It hovers and lets you know that it's there when you need it. It's the same way for drug users. The users feel that same hovering presence. They know it's there when needed.

At twelve years old, I began taking steps to ensure my future wealth. The way I looked at it was a simple game of supply and demand. The addicts demanded

Falling Into Your Purpose

what I supplied and they supplied the cash for the things I desired. It was the cycle of life.

At first my grandparents had no clue about what I was doing. They knew I was never home and had basically stopped going to school, but there wasn't much they could do to change my ways.

My little brother and I continued living with them while my mother went in and out of drug houses looking for the next fix that would keep her reality on mute. I can only imagine the heaviness we all placed on the hearts of my grandparents. My mother, my uncle, and I were all hell on wheels. My mission was to lighten their load and start taking care of my little brother and myself. I never wanted to be a burden to my grandparents. So I turned my hustle up and became self-sufficient.

My dudes and I were all about the cash, the clothes, and the chics. The lifestyle I was living comes with side effects. I don't know many that enter it and come out unscathed. The good times are immeasurable but when the bad side of the game begins to show up there's hell to pay.

Reality began giving me a glimpse of what my life could turn out to be. But I didn't take heed. The money was too good for me to walk away from. I was living the life of a grown hustler and I loved it. That is until the grown man consequences kicked in.

Getting into territory battles and staying on top of those that tried playing me like a kid was an everyday thing. But when a squabble gone wrong between one of my best friends and another guy from the neighborhood happened, life got real.

Most of us are kids that grew up way too fast.

Sophia Janell Taylor

Inside of my arms is where he took his last breath. And it was all over nothing.

My boys and I had gone out to the club that night just to celebrate life. Everything was always good as long as we were getting money.

Out of the clear blue, a dispute between my friend and the security guard started then we all rushed in. A gun was pulled out. There was a tussle for it, and the rest is history.

At fifteen years old, I had a front row seat to life and death. I watched my best friend's existence disappear like the last peek of the sun going down over the horizon. The worse feeling of it all was that I couldn't do anything to save him. It was the most devastating thing I'd ever experienced.

The heaviness of the world plopped down in my lap and took up residency. The life I was living had a trap door and I was in too deep to walk away. I never wanted any repercussions to fall on my grandparents, so I decided it was time to move out. I was only fifteen, but felt I was ready to turn up my grown man game. Despite the warning whispers from the streets. I carried on as if I hadn't heard a thing.

I bought my first car with cash and no license. It had to be titled in my friends name because I wasn't old enough to drive. I continued living life in the fast lane.

I partnered with an older street connect in the hood and took my hustle to another level. Between the chics, the toys, and the clothes, I was spending so much money until I often didn't see what I made. It was a crazy cycle that was spinning out of control. My conscience would speak to me periodically but still I carried on. I could see it all going wrong one day. But until then, I planned on living life like there was no tomorrow.

I always wished I could've lived a normal teenage life, but I didn't have a normal start. When I was younger, I imagined being an actor. I didn't know how it would happen, but I saw it in my mind. The deeper I got in the game, the more I wanted to be free. I loved the money, but I didn't want the drama. I wanted something different but I didn't know who to reach out to. I wanted somebody to save me from myself and from the streets.

My admiration for several television characters led me to write to them in hopes of getting a response. I went to the library and did some research. I thought I'd found my heroes' home addresses and knew if they heard the cry of a young boy from the inner city they'd come to my rescue. I wrote Bill Cosby, Elizabeth Taylor and Michael J. Foxx. I pled my case and poured my soul out to them in the letter. Although my reading and writing skills were horrible, I did the best I could. I told them that I was a big drug dealer and how I wanted to become an actor but didn't know how to go about it. All I needed was an opportunity.

I hoped one of them would respond and reach their hand out to pull me up and out of the slums. I wanted them to come to the rescue of a little boy that had dreams and drive the size of the world. I always had drive. I just didn't know where to put it. My naivety led me to believe that they'd respond. I just knew that one day they'd come and rescue me. But they never did. Nobody ever came.

From then on, it was all or nothing for me. My reckless moves continued. My grandparents definitely knew what I was doing by this time. They tried passing advice on to me but I was young and headstrong. I didn't listen. I continued my hustle, gaining ground and making my mark in the streets.

One day while visiting my grandparents the phone rang and I answered it. My mothers' voice was on the other end asking to speak to my grandfather. Her voice had such a frantic tone to it. I asked her what was wrong but nothing could've ever prepared me for what she shared.

"They raped me!" she yelled out. "They raped me!"

My heart took a dive into my stomach and my anger shot through the roof.

"Who raped you?" I asked. "Mama, who raped you?"

She explained the situation to me and that was it. I already knew what the end was going to look like.

My mother's lifestyle wasn't a secret. Everyone in my neighborhood knew her vices. Those closest to her could always tell her truths from her lies. When she ran down the specifics of the scenario, I unfortunately knew she was telling the truth. I always knew when she was telling the truth.

Her confession opened up wounds from both of our pasts. Not long before this incident happened, she revealed to me that I was a product of rape. All of those years I'd been longing to know who my father was, where he was, and why he hadn't been in my life flew out the window after she revealed the story to me.

At a young age, she endured being violated. To make matters worse, she held it all in for so many years. I no longer wondered about the mysterious missing father. She cleared it all up. She was only thirteen years old when it happened the first time and here it is almost seventeen years later, coming back to open up unhealed scars.

Regardless of the vices of your loved ones, nobody wants to see them abused or taken advantage of. Some may say her lifestyle put her in that predicament.

Others would've waited on the law to handle the situation. My young mind led me to act out on pure emotions.

Until you're standing in the shoes as a woman's son hearing something as horrific as this, you will never know how you would react.

When anger rises, think of the consequences.
-Confucius

A few days had passed but my emotions were still on high. The memory of my mother's confession about how I was conceived played over and over in my head. The cries she let out and the description of the ways in which they violated her made my blood boil over. She was broken beyond repair.

When I finally found out where the guys lived, I knew I would be making a visit. I didn't have the balance or the maturity to simmer or analyze the consequences. I didn't really think long or hard about the outcome. I just knew my mother was scared and hurting. Her emotions were my emotions. We were connected.

If you asked me if I thought she deserved a mother of the year award, I'd say "No." Did I think she deserved to be violated to the point of going into hiding and breaking down between every sentence? "No." And did I believe the authorities would bring justice to the situation? "Hell No!"

A few days after hearing my mother's sorrowful confession I went over to my grand parents house to get the weapon I'd been hiding in their basement. I ran down the stairs and straight to my hiding spot then heard my grandmother call out my name.

"Bring up the laundry from the dryer."

"Yes ma'am.' I replied.

I brought the basket up and sat it down. Just as I stood up the gun fell out of my pocket. She looked down at the floor then looked back up at me.

"What are you gonna do with that?"

I just stood there with a dumb look on my face.

"Wannie, sit down. Let me talk to you." I knew a speech that was gonna go in one ear and out of the other was coming. My rage was beyond calming. Everything was such a blur after hearing my mother's voice. I just didn't understand how anybody could violate a human being the way my mother had been violated.

My grandmother's advice mumbled in the distance. It felt like I was there, but I really wasn't. I truly believe I had mentally checked out.

"Baby don't go and do anything that will get you in the kind of trouble that you can't get out of. Wannie, there's only two places you're gonna go. That's either the cemetery or prison. Either one of them is gonna kill my soul. Baby, let the police handle it. Listen to me sweetheart. Just let the police handle it."

Emotional responses causes regretful behavior, while thinking gives you time to simmer and evaluate.

Later that night, I was at the door of one of the men's house that raped my mother. I knocked on the door and he answered it. I told him who I was, then I asked him if he knew my mother and if he and his friends had raped her. He flew off the handle and made a few threatening accusations towards my mother and I. He reached for his then I reached for mine. The next thing I knew, I was in a courtroom with both of our heartbroken families crying their eyes out for different reasons.

When you get down to it, most things are a matter of choice!

Twenty-two years and no more than fifty for 2nd degree murder is what they sentenced me to. It didn't take long for regret to settle in. His family's cries echoed in my ears and tore me apart. I had taken the life of somebody's child, brother, father, cousin, uncle and friend. I played God by taking his life and I was about to pay the consequences for my actions.

My family's heartbreak weighed so heavy on my heart. The very thing I'd been trying to avoid was staring me in my face. I never wanted to be a burden to my grandparents. I only wanted to stand on my own two feet and take care of my little brother and I. I never imagined this becoming my life.

I was only seventeen years old with a 7th grade education. That sounds crazy to admit but it's the truth. I had so many regrets that I couldn't shake. Some of them I could change, others I couldn't.

The best thing I could do with my time was educate myself. It didn't take long for me to figure out that everything I thought I knew, I didn't. I became a student of all kinds. I figured I had the time, so I might as well spend it learning skills I needed to get through life. I began teaching myself how to read and spell correctly. After all, I'd only gotten to the 7th grade, and I hadn't soaked much up in those years.

There were several things I did everyday without fail. I worked out. I studied. I thought about my family

Sophia Janell Taylor

and I prayed that God and the mother of the man's life I'd taken would forgive me.

Time in prison seemed to move slowly. I survived by accepting my fate and living in the now. I had a long way to go until I set foot on free land again, and I knew if I constantly thought about being free I would go crazy. So instead, I created a formula for survival and I let the years take care of themselves.

Every time a new kid came into the system, my heart would go out to him. I always felt bad for them because they reminded me of myself. They were young, immature, and clueless.

I learned that prison is a society within itself. There are rules and traditions that you have to learn and abide by in order to survive. Just like the streets, I don't know too many that come out unscathed. I've been in knife fights, fist fights, food fights and everything in between. I've seen horrible things happen that I wouldn't wish on anyone.

As the years went by, my book knowledge grew along with my survival skills. Although I was knocking down my time, I really missed my family and I hated being away from my little brother. The fact that my grandparents weren't getting any younger constantly gnawed at me. I kept praying that they'd be alive and well when I returned home.

My grandfather would drive hours away just to lay his eyes on me and give me encouraging words. I always looked forward to our time together. On one of his visits in 1993, he informed me that he'd been diagnosed with cancer. He continued visiting me until the treatments took control of his body.

On October 2, 1994, he made his transition from this earth. I couldn't help but think that the stress of my situation was partly to blame. I understand that we've all got an expiration date. I guess I just wanted more time with him.

I continued chopping down my sentence day-by-day and week-by-week until my time was completed.

I served a total of 19 years and 8 months in correctional facilities. In 2010, I was released from prison and finally back home with a burning desire to make the world a better place.

What I know now to be true is the power of prayer. I know for a fact that it's the only way I made it through those years.

Trust me in your times of trouble and I will rescue you, and you will give me glory.
-Psalm 50:15

When I returned home to my family back home with my family nothing seemed the same. There was a drastic difference in my neighborhood. It felt like a plague had taken over the entire city. It looked like a bomb had crashed down on it, that's how bad it was.

Most of the friends I ran with back in the day were either incarcerated, dead or had relocated. The worst change of all was that my grandfather was no longer alive.

I fumbled my way through the streets of my old community putting pieces of my life back together again. My grandparents were always my pillars of strength, and though it may have appeared as if I wasn't listening to them while coming up, I could never escape their voices.

2011 was a bittersweet year for me. God gave me one of the best blessings I could've ever imagined, then he took one away. I married the love of my life but soon after, I lost the strongest pillar I've ever had.

Sophia Janell Taylor

I think my grandmother held on just long enough to see me released. That unconditional love I always felt from her was suddenly gone. She left me, but she'll forever live inside of my heart. The devastation of her passing is still beyond anything I can express. I'm just grateful that I was able to spend a little time with her before she made her transition.

My determination to succeed and make my grandparents proud of me became my daily focus. I had been educating and preparing myself for life after incarceration for almost two decades. It was now time to put the lessons to work. There were so many things I wanted to do. I realized how far behind I was and I knew I had to play the game of "catching up."

By any means necessary, I was determined to make a difference in my community.

One of the harshest realities of being an ex-convict is experiencing roadblocks everywhere you turn. Once you return back to your community, the rules and stipulations they have in place keep ex-felons painted in a corner. It's one of the most confusing and sabotaging systems I've ever seen.

The high percentage of ex-convicts that return back into their communities are usually unable to find employment because of the road blocks placed on them. What do they expect the outcome to be if you can't get a job? You guessed it. They expect you to do something dumb to survive so you'll return back into the system.

The Center for Human Rights found that 76% of former inmates said finding work after being released was difficult or nearly impossible.

Thankfully, I was working and making my way through it all but I was aware of the fact that every

Falling Into Your Purpose

head inside of those prison walls brings big money. It's the very reason why the focus isn't placed on rehabilitation or successful integration back into society. It's the reason that the doors to the prisons continue to revolve.

For many former inmates, the solution to getting ahead after prison is to skip the interview process altogether and start their own business.

The process of finding work and the cries from my fallen community sparked something inside of me. I wanted to do whatever I could to make a difference. I wanted to find a solution for the problems that appeared to be getting worse.

Everything was so different from when I left. There were so many schools and factories closed. We didn't have any grocery stores left in the neighborhood. Abandoned houses seemed to be blooming like dandelions. There were only a handful of fire stations left and they had laid off so many police officers till people in the city knew they could get away with just about anything. It had become a war zone and the cries from the citizens seemed to be falling on deaf ears.

One of my prayers while incarcerated was that God would send me home to do something so miraculous that there be no question that it was him that made it come to pass.

In 2012, I was officially released from parole and soon after I turned my name in as a candidate to become the 5th Ward City Councilman.

You should've seen the looks and heard the comments I received. Both were priceless. Many people thought I'd lost my mind. "Didn't you just get out of prison?" Most said or thought to themselves. But the past didn't matter to me. I was looking ahead and listening to a call that was greater than my past mistakes.

Perception is everything and I made a choice to look at my past as an asset and not a liability.

The only time you should look back should be to see how far you've come.

For eight months straight I poured my heart and soul into my campaign. I knocked on doors from sun up to sun down connecting with every citizen in my neighborhood. It had been years since a member of council had shown up at their doorstep to get their take on what they needed. It was such a humbling and heartfelt experience.

The people in the community just want to be heard. They want to live in a peaceful environment that supports their needs. And they want to be represented by a person that truly cares. They don't want the frills and the unnecessary propaganda that comes with politicians. They want a real person that they can relate to.

I didn't have the money, the campaign headquarters, the staff or the backing from name brand people. Sometimes my wife and her girlfriend pitched in and knocked on doors with me but for the most part it was me, myself and God, and we were on a mission.

I just wanted to be a voice for the people. I wanted to see the city create programs that included the forgotten ones. If we could just reach out and connect to the young people that wreak havoc on the community and give them opportunities, we could put an end to this cycle.

My heart goes out to everybody, but it really goes out to the underprivileged and the ex-convicts that really want to change and make a difference in society.

Falling Into Your Purpose

I'm determined to do my part to start a movement of change.

In 2013, I managed to unseat the incumbent and become the first person in the United States of America to hold a public office after being convicted of 2nd degree murder. I feel as though this entire journey has had nothing to do with me.

The victory was proof of God's favor and it gave people like me a spark of hope. Sometimes all we need to see is a simple spark to carry on.

If my story isn't a testimony of falling into your purpose, I don't know what is. I went from being a product of rape, a hellion in the streets, to being incarcerated and elected as a City Councilman.

In 2014, I started my own cleaning service and now I'm able to provide employment opportunities for people that society has tried to hold back.

I wish I could tell you that it was my hard work that put me where I'm at today, but I can't. I refuse to take any credit for what God is doing in my life. I can feel him moving things around for me every day and I'm beyond grateful for his mercy and his forgiveness. He is a God of second chances and I spread my testimony everywhere I go.

God created you to do amazing things!
-Ephesians 2:10

Those that tried to deter me or speak negatively about my bid for council added fuel to my fire. I'm more determined now than I was before to create change. I know I won't be able to fix every foul thing about the workings of the system, but I'm definitely going to make my mark.

In 2010, 28% of my community had felonies on their records. I'm sure it's much higher now.

Sophia Janell Taylor

Nevertheless my mission is to change laws for ex-convicts that have turned their lives around and paid their debt to society. I want to create programs for the underprivileged to get the skills they need to get better jobs so they can provide better lives for themselves and their children.

All of these things make a difference in communities and in the world. I am determined to create change.

Every day I work towards equality and productivity for my community. I'm finally living in my purpose. My constituents know that I do everything I can to fight for them because I can relate to them. On so many levels, I am them.

Before I formed you in the womb, I knew you.
-Jeremiah 1:5

Falling Into Your Purpose

**No matter what your past looks like, tomorrow is a new day.
Whatever you see your life being is possible, as long as you believe.**

Sophia Janell Taylor

MY SURVIVAL TIPS

1. Fasting promotes discipline.

2. Pray and strengthen your faith.

3. Take things one day at a time.

4. Educate and prepare yourself for life outside of prison.

5. Stay positive

PURPOSE PAUSE

*Writing is therapy.

*Live in the now.

*Look at your past as an asset, not a liability.

*Look ahead and listen to a call greater than your past mistakes.

*Work towards equality and productivity for your community.

*Work for a cause bigger than yourself.

*Have unshakeable belief.

*Forgive yourself.

F.I.Y.P Workbook Questions

Falling Into Your Purpose

1. If you could do anything in the world, what would it be?

_____
_____
_____
_____
_____
_____
_____
_____
_____
_____
_____
_____
_____
_____
_____

Sophia Janell Taylor

2. On a scale of 1 to 5, how badly do you want to experience this?

5   4   3   2   1

Falling Into Your Purpose

3. What do you need to get started?

_____
_____
_____
_____
_____
_____
_____
_____
_____
_____
_____
_____
_____
_____
_____
_____

Sophia Janell Taylor

4. On a scale of 1 to 5, how happy would you be if you could experience what you've been dreaming of?

5   4   3   2   1

5. What do you believe is hindering you from experiencing your dreams?

Sophia Janell Taylor

6. Name your 5 best qualities.

1.

2.

3.

4.

5.

Falling Into Your Purpose

7. Name 5 things you love doing.

1.

2.

3.

4.

5.

Sophia Janell Taylor

8. How often do you do things you love to do?

Very often   Often   Rarely   Never

9. What obstacles from your past have kept you stuck on repeat?

Sophia Janell Taylor

**The happiest people live in today not yesterday nor tomorrow. The gift of life lies in today.
That's why it's called "the present."**

10. Name 5 things you love most about yourself.

1.

2.

3.

4.

5.

Sophia Janell Taylor

11. Name 5 things you would like to become by utilizing your best qualities.

1.

2.

3.

4.

5.

12. Name 2 things you would like to achieve in the next year.

1.
_____
_____
_____
_____

2.
_____
_____
_____
_____

3.
_____
_____
_____
_____

Sophia Janell Taylor

13. Name 3 things you need to do to achieve your goals.

1.

_____
_____
_____
_____

2.

_____
_____
_____
_____

3.

_____
_____
_____
_____

14. What would you like your legacy to be?

15. Write 5 things you'll begin doing that will help you to finally move forward. (i.e. counseling, forgiving yourself/others, volunteering, prayer, meditation.)

1. _____

2. _____

3. _____

4. _____

5. _____

Falling Into Your Purpose

Journaling your past experiences then burying the journal afterwards sometimes aids in turning the channel when your mind wants to play the same show.

16. What would you like to tell your younger self?

17. What would you tell the present "you" that would help to keep you motivated and moving forward?

_____
_____
_____
_____
_____
_____
_____
_____
_____
_____
_____
_____
_____
_____
_____
_____
_____

Sophia Janell Taylor

***Visualizing and speaking positivity over yourself is a great start to creating the life of your dreams.**

Falling Into Your Purpose

Stop yourself from negative thinking and speaking. This small change can make a big difference.

Sophia Janell Taylor

We are the only ones that can build what we see our life being. We truly are the architect of our lives.

18. What did you learn from these stories?

_____

_____

_____

_____

_____

_____

_____

_____

_____

_____

_____

_____

_____

_____

_____

_____

Sophia Janell Taylor

Periodic bumps along the journey of life is guaranteed. I believe they're placed there to make us better people. Turning trials into triumph depends on our thoughts and our words, which triggers our emotions and ultimately our success or failure.

Falling Into Your Purpose

What we think and speak is controlled by us. Many think it's more complex than that and perhaps it is. The bottom line of life is: It will always be what we say and believe it to be. ☺

Sophia Janell Taylor

Each and every one of us has a back story. Whether good, bad, joyous or difficult, we've all experienced things that could hinder our entire lives. The key words here are "could hinder." Life isn't about what we've been through, it's about what we do with our experiences.

Falling Into Your Purpose

The magic is in what you build from your journey, who you touch by the brilliance of your outcome and the outlook you choose to carry throughout your days.

Sophia Janell Taylor

By no means should we ever diminish the scenes from our past. Yet, they should be put in their proper place therefore allowing light to shine on the beauty and newness of today.

Falling Into Your Purpose

The only light shining on the past is the light you continue to hold. There's a reason for your fall. There's a reason for it all. You've just got to figure out how to turn it all into your purpose.
                                -Sophia Janell Taylor

Sophia Janell Taylor

As long as you have breath in your body, you have an opportunity to start again. ☺

Falling Into Your Purpose

Thank you for reading. I pray that these stories have found their way to your heart and mind. May your soul be healed and your tomorrows be filled with health, joy, possibilities, dreams, loads of laughter and all the love you can hold and share.
Sincerely,
-Sophia Janell Taylor

Sophia Janell Taylor

If you or someone you know has an example of turning tragedy into triumph, please feel free to contact us at sagacioususblishing@yahoo.com. We welcome the inspiration.

About The Author

Sophia Janell Taylor is the creator and host of the show Rehabin The Hood. She's also a bestselling author, recording artist, community investor, activist and public motivator. She's found a way to combine her love for artistic expression and business through her many ventures. She dedicates much of her time inspiring others to find their passion and turn it into their purpose.

www.ingramcontent.com/pod-product-compliance
Lightning Source LLC
Chambersburg PA
CBHW020936090426
42736CB00010B/1164